DEATH
OR
GLORY

A GENTLEMAN
EXPLORER'S
GUIDE TO
MANLINESS,
MOUNTAINEERING
& MORE

Dr. Horace S. Browntrout

To Dave,
may you find
your destiny on
the mountain of
omanliness!
Best,
Dr. Browntrout

TABLE OF CONTENTS

EXCERPTS &
PITHY QUOTES

ON DETERMINATION

Do you want that mountain? Then go out and take it, bite off a piece of it. Spit out the piece. Bite off another piece. Spit that piece out, until the entire mountain is nothing but pea-sized rubble. Are you going to whine because you might lose a few teeth in the process, or are you going to spit out the blood and your teeth, and keep biting with whatever you have left? That is steely resolve.

———◆———

Mountains are for the strong. Mountains are for the hard. Mountains are for men with iron in their blood, fists of granite, eyes of flinty resolve!

———◆———

To make juice, one must beat the orange to a pulp and squeeze the life out of it. As with oranges, so it is with mountains.

———◆———

Are all of your arms and legs broken after plunging into the crevasse, or are you simply having a bout of unmanliness preventing your hard climb out of the jaws of the abyss?

———◆———

If a panda bear bites off both of your arms and one leg, that still leaves one good leg you can use as a weapon to smite your furry enemy. That is character. That is resolve. That is determination. That is class.

It is only in a molten bath of steely resolve that the spirit of man is honed to perfection once the mortal frame has been burned away, and all that remains is its purity of essence, a sharpened, gleaming, stabbing weapon, a thing made to subdue other things.

ON CHARACTER

You cannot build character. Character is forged, not built. How is character forged? It is forged in a bath of steely resolve.

ON COWARDICE

The coward is a man without mastery. He gets his ideas out of fancy books that tell him to worry about everything. He takes no action, but dithers over every decision.

ON CHILD REARING

If yours is a pretty but petulant young lass who is difficult to please, buy her a pony and name it Strawberry. Inform the girl that if she is not right and good while you are gone, Strawberry will be killed and fed to the yeti. If such an unfortunate state of events comes to pass, explain to your daughter, "Strawberry is now an angel who frolics in Pony Heaven, a much, much less cruel place than a yeti cave. Dry your tears, girl child. You will thank me later."

———◆———

Tell Dolly that daddy thinks Butterscotch is a fine name

for a pony, a real dandy of a name. Tell her to take
real good care of Butterscotch, and to empty out his
litterbox everyday, because until daddy can come home
Butterscotch will be a pony angel who takes good care
of those girls.

Beat your spawn at regular intervals. Use a switch, a rod,
cudgel, cane, or a heavy, leaded pipe. Rap the knuckles,
smack the bare bottom, box their ears, or brain them if they
attempt to run.

Remember, a good father never hits out of anger, but only
with love—even when he is enraged.

Offer your child a toy bear with a ticking clock stuffed
inside. Explain that "Spreckles" the bear is very angry, and
has a bomb inside his tummy. Speckles loves daddy, and
will watch over and take notes on everything the children do
whilst daddy is away in the Himalaya, and if they're bad,
his stomach will explode, killing everyone and sending them
to hell.

Wanton self-abuse has turned many a lad with a bright
future into a drooling idiot suitable only for the
lunatic asylum.

It is best the a loving father instill his authority from an
early age, insisting that his children refer to him as

Colonel, Leftenant, or sir. A father, in turn should refer to his children only by Mr. or Ms. combined with last name. This is an excellent way of cutting out extra mollycoddling that can weaken a child's natural agression and will to survive.

ON KEEN ADVICE TO MAIDENLY DAUGHTERS

Do remember your kegels, and clench tightly, for poisonous gonads lurk in the night, just beyond your walls. Only the staunchest defense may prevent them from kidnapping you and turning your temple of purity into a house of ill repute.

Remember girl, your booty is Satan's bounty.

ON MANAGING ONE'S WIFE

When not engaging female guests or adjusting her toilette, the explorer's wife should be pining for the explorer's loving, intrepid, intimidatingly manly presence at all times.

ON SUBDUING THE YETI

On occasion, the yeti may be placated by the use of a female yeti decoy, sprayed with copious amounts of musky female yeti estrous scent. As the males attempt to compete for the privilege of mating with the decoy, the expedition leader can deploy a man deep into the yeti cave to dig for gold.

If a yeti attacks from behind, make eye contact with the rogue, and use the power of animal magnetism to sedate it, then take off its head with one, deft swipe from the katana. Then find the beast's nest and slay its entire brood.

Be especially wary of the wily yeti, or snow-daemon. He may attempt to arouse your sympathies, but he is rouge and a scamp, and he will attempt to bedevil you with primate trickery.

When given half a chance, the yeti will not hesitate to eat you, so therefore consider yourself at liberty to eat the yeti when deemed expedient or appropriate.

Advice to the yeti: You will be given one hour of puppy time for every troy ounce of gold we remove for your treasure cave. You must never eat the puppies during puppy time.

ON THE USES OF EXPEDITIONARY PENGUINS

Of course, you do realize that penguins have culinary and spiritual needs that must be attended to.

Each morning, every penguin regiment must rise for the raising of the Union Jack, and chirp their best rendition of God Save the Queen as best they can.

All penguins will kneel, fold their flippers, and praise Jesus as best their limited squeaks and grunts will allow. All those who shirk prayers or are seen worshipping the penguin fish god will be beaten and eaten.

Be sure that you have at least a few lactating females around, for nothing is sweeter than tea flavored with penguin milk. Each penguin should yield about one pint of penguin milk per day, quite enough to supply the gentlemen, the puppies, and the kitty cats of the perilous expedition into the unknown.

All penguins should be trained to tuck explorers into bed at night, and to clean up after the puppies. They should be able to beguile with their silly antics, balance red rubber balls on their beaks, but also able to shoulder a pack at a moment's notice, and take up arms against the yeti.

ON THE CARE AND USES OF OTHER EXPEDITIONARY MAMMALS

The horse may be viewed as a walking, neighing meat stick with legs and hooves. Every effort should be made to secure horse meat for the penguins, the men, and the puppies, as well as the kitty cats, who often say, "meow likes a big, fat horsey steak."

Along with the cats, a supply of rats and rabbits should be brought up the mountain, for nothing so occupies a mischievous pussy than chasing a rat around a glacier.

What rugged, careworn chap wouldn't like to see a docile bunny face peeking through his tent flaps each morning whilst he takes his morning glass of penguin milk.

ON SUBDUING NATURE

The wildness of creatures is what makes them unpredictable, foolish, and prone to attack. Do not wait for a warning sign. A gentleman always forms ranks and brandishes his weapon, challenging offensive creatures to a civilized duel.

ON EXPLORATION

But what of the rest of us, born of the slums, denizens of the middle-class ghetto? Do we who do not have our slippery fingers on the fickle teats of the Money Cow have any chance to avoid the horrors of a debtors' prison upon our return from the summit?

ON DEATH

Step over the dead ones and continue on, knowing that you went further and lasted longer than your deceased brethren conquerors. The mountain gods have smote them and they have their eye on you too. The vultures hover ever closer, waiting their turn to pry your tight flesh out of the trendy neon orange goose down jacket that flaps around your lifeless body in the cruel wind. Your day will come.

———

All gentlemen pursuing manly endeavors accept death as the probable outcome, and consider survival secondary to the goal of struggling with honor against the force of nature.

———◆———

Until the evil gods make cruel sport of your ragged skeleton, stand up and shake your fist at them. Step over the corpses of the weak, the meek and the mild, not somberly, but with self-adoration and confidence!

ON GLORY

Once a summit is bagged, the end of the rainbow is reached and like a mischievous leprechaun stealing a pot of gold, you too may dance a conquering jig whilst imitating the sound of flatulence.

———◆———

Manhood lies in wresting from the gods the freedom that was always intended to be the birthright of man.

———◆———

Glory resides in the struggle for freedom, in the test of will, in the tapping of all reserves, in taxing one's strength and resolve to the upper limits of their capabilities. Live or die, what does it matter? Mountaineers and gentlemen were never intended to reach a venerable age.

———◆———

Glory comes only at the moment when death seems imminent, yet for some reason the road veers slightly to the right instead of the left. The falling boulder misses by an inch. The yawning abyss roars like a feral tiger, but does not pull the sojourner into its unforgiving maw.

By placing his spiked boot prints on the tops of mountains, Man holds himself firm, erect against the will of the gods. He contends for their immortality by stealing their Glory.

It is absolutely imperative that you carve your name and titles into the stone face nearest the summit with the time, date and length and girth of your penis in metric as well as standard measurements.

Once at the top, the expedition leader should fall to his stomach and begin pelvic-thrusting against the top of the mountain.

Will you comport yourself like a flaccid, sneaky scoundrel or will you beat the mountain into submission, bending millions of tons of rock and ice to conform to the dictates of your will, like a gentleman? Practice your pelvic thrusts. Remember your steely resolve. Swing high your axe. Never shed one tear. Don't ever masturbate. Keep pulling the trigger, and you too may one day find your destiny of death or glory that awaits every man on top of every mountain.

ON MAN'S PLACE IN NATURE

Man is two things. He is an outcast. He is a killer. He is an animal. Man is the apex predator in every food chain, a chain wrapped round the throat of all ecology.

ON MANLINESS

A man must remember to not place acetone or lye on his nipples, for the resulting caustic burns and outrageous swelling could delay the expedition by a month or more.

———+———

White men may not always be the right men, as those lads with the pasty white skin of the stay-at-home may have never been tested against our enemy, Mother Nature.

ON THE QUALITIES OF THE LEADER

Your gonads should be twice the weight of the next man's stones. They must leave a distinct pattern as they trail through the dirt betwixt your solid, oaken legs. You must stand always with your feet as far apart as possible, hands on hips or waving in the air. When you speak, your whisper should be louder than the next loudest man's shout. Your gesticulations should be sweeping and dramatic when addressing the men. You should stare into the eyes of each man until he lowers his gaze respectfully. Each step you take should shake the ground beneath you. When not engaged in other purposeful activity, your hands should be balled into fists, always ready to strike at the first sign of adversity or insubordination. Your aggressive, dominant stance will be of the greatest comfort to the men. If words don't work, try fists. Or at least use threatening or intimidating gestures to get your point across. Draw your katana, and wave it around. This will let him know who the boss is.

ON TERRITORIALITY

A line in the snow should be drawn around your camp,
so that any who encroach on the camp space without
permission may fairly meet with severe corporal punishment.
A member of the party should stand guard at all hours with
a drawn katana to enforce this edict. Mark the boundaries
of your camp or your territory with a stream of urine.

ON DISPLAYS OF AFFECTION
BETWEEN MEN

The vertical bro hug allows for weight-shifting away from
the center of the bro, and the operation of normal survival
reflexes that naturally tend to repulse physical affection
between men.

ON EUTHANASIA

If, after imbibing three tablespoons of Mrs. Right-A-Way's
Tincture of Opium Cure All and a shot to the head fail to
achieve the desired effect, then bury the victim in snow,
making him as comfortable as possible.

———◆———

If the dying man can conjure no final words as best befits
the profundity of his impending demise, recommend that
he refer to Dr. Browntrout's Unabridged Guide to Suggested
Last Words and Final Statements For the Doomed, the
Damned and the Dying.

ON THE UNMANLINESS
OF SUPPLIMENTAL OXYGEN

Gentlemen breathe whatever air they encounter, whether that be ground air, or hydrogen sulfide belched out of volcanic vents. Real men do not wince at the idea of inhaling a bit of thin, crisp air now and then. It adds vigor to the spirit!

ON QUANTIFYING ONE'S OWN MANHOOD

Another proven measure of strength is the length and girth of your penis. Two inches wide by eight inches long while flaccid is the minimum requirement. You can measure your penis with measuring tape, but do not artificially stretch or pull your member because that's cheating. Total scrotal sac weight (TSSW) – (right testicle + left testicle) x total hair covered body surface (THCBS) = manliness.

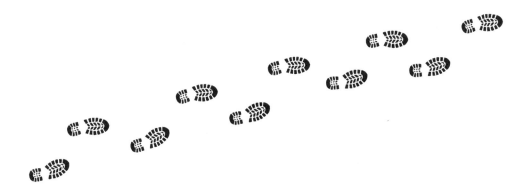

PROLOGUE

Come friend, you too must die. Why moan about it so?
Even Patroclus died, a far, far better man than you.
And look, you see how handsome and powerful I am?
The son of a great man, the mother who gave me
life a deathless goddess. But even for me,
I tell you, death and the strong force of fate are waiting.

—The Illiad. Book 21, Achilles fights the river.

In 2003, the author of this book assembled an expedition and ascended Pilot Knob, at 1,450 feet, the second-highest point in Iowa, and in 2007 he ascended Eagle Mountain, at 2,301 feet, the highest point in Minnesota. In 2002, the author ascended Timm's Hill, highest point in Wisconsin at 1,951.5 feet. These feats of mountaineering were accomplished alpine style, without the use of supplemental oxygen, without any time for acclimatization, and without any equipment save a walking stick and an angry girlfriend. Despite these achievements, the author feels that the best way to learn to climb mountains is to not climb any mountains at all, but to read about mountaineering in a book, and then leave home and hope behind to meet your destiny in the most manly fashion possible.

ON DEATH AND GLORY

Glory seldom goes to the living; nor does it automatically go to the dead. The road to death runs parallel to the path to Glory. The true adventurer has a foot on each path without even realizing it. For the living, Glory comes only at the moment when death seems imminent, yet for some reason the road veers slightly to the right instead of the left. The falling boulder misses by an inch. The yawning abyss roars like a feral tiger, but does not pull the sojourner into its unforgiving maw.

The gentleman explorer accepts his fate gladly, whatever it may be. Destiny cleaves us to life by a thin cord, and death is the fate of all. The real man says: So be it. I'm ready. To prepare for the final hour is to labor beneath the delusion that we can predict when it will come.

To accept the mystery of fate is to reject the fear that ensues from attempting to control it. All gentlemen pursuing manly endeavors accept death as the probable outcome, and consider survival secondary to the goal of struggling with honor against the force of nature. To test one's will against that of the universe, to throw one's mortal frame into combat against the forces of the eternal is to discover who you are and what real men are made of.

Mountains are the homes of the gods. Everything of value to man was stolen from the gods, in hard-won struggle. Although we may not be the architects of our own destinies, we can still shirk our role as passive playthings of the gods. Manhood lies in wresting from the gods the freedom that was always intended to be the birthright of man. To live free and die free is the penultimate manly endeavor.

Therefore, man fearlessly, intrepidly ventures forth onto the mountain, attempting to reach its summit—the mere act of making the attempt is to spite the cruel gods who make sport of our suffering. Glory does not reside in claiming the summit, in living to tell the tale or in dying a lonely death on the mountain far from friends and family. Rather, Glory resides in the struggle for freedom, in the test of will, in the tapping of all reserves, in taxing one's strength and resolve to the upper limits of their capabilities. Live or die, what does it matter? Mountaineers and gentlemen were never intended to reach a venerable age. A candle burns longer than a bonfire, but the bonfire shines brightest.

Let your resolve be the gasoline you pour on the bonfire of your efforts to wrest Glory from the cruel gods who mock us. Leave the candle lighting for the weak. Let all the dandies and milksops be the ones who light candles at your funeral pyre; let them be the tellers of your tales; let fumbling, bumbling fops be the ones who return to their warm beds each night to rub their soft bellies. Mountains are for the strong. Mountains are for the hard. Mountains are for men with iron in their blood, fists of granite, eyes of flinty resolve!

WHAT MAKES A MAN A MAN?

*...every specific body strives to become master
over all space and to extend its force...
and to thrust back all that resists its extension.*

—Friedrich Nietzsche, The Will To Power

Man is two things. He is an outcast. He is a killer. He is
an animal. Man is the apex predator in every food chain,
a chain wrapped round the throat of all ecology. The only
thing separating man from beast is the fact that man can
kill from afar by means of firearms, while beast cannot. A
gentleman is not a gentle man, but rather he is a man un-

afraid of conquest, unafraid of spilling blood for gold and Glory. He will sacrifice his own life on the holy alter of ambition and Glory. He will help the weak, for so long as the weak exist the strong may have their tales told, and the incorporeal spirits of the strong—kept alive by the force of their indomitable wills—may revel in their posthumous Glory.

For the tomb of man will never hold fast his spirit! Stripped of bone, muscle and flesh, nothing remains of man but his steely resolve. It is only in a molten bath of steely resolve that the spirit of man is honed to perfection once the mortal frame has been burned away, and all that remains is its purity of essence, a sharpened, gleaming, stabbing weapon, a thing made to subdue other things.

Man the outcast is both the weapon and the wielder of the weapon. He who would call himself a man knows too, that despite his position—or because of it—he is loathed by all that lives. He who hunts would easily be hunted. The cruel gods who gave us these gifts, mock our nakedness, our utter helplessness in the face of the enormous indifference of nature. Nature hates our every breath. Nature plots our doom at a thousand turns. Man must either subdue and conquer nature, or be destroyed by her. And therefore, man is an outcast and an outlaw. Endowed with consciousness, man has been elevated beyond the gladiator pit of evolution's struggle for survival—but just barely so.

The only solution is to best the gods by becoming gods. The first step in usurping the gods is to violate their sanctuary on earth. By placing his spiked boot prints on the tops of mountains, Man holds himself firm, erect against the will of the gods. He contends for their immortality by stealing their Glory.

Man now reigns supreme, but only from afar, only alone, no longer a brother to other creatures, but their enemy and master. It is this struggle for mastery in the environment that shaped us that dares us, implores us, compels us to conquer the mountain. It is only through conquest of the mountain that the spirit of man can coexist with his living flesh.

A PROPER EXPEDITIONARY COIF

It goes without saying that part of what makes a man manly, is his general state of hirsutism. No man should depart for a proper expedition without a coif and the kit for its maintenance that best befits his merits as a man.

Proper business always is executed at the top of the head, and therefore mud flaps, pompadours, lion's manes, skullets and Diggly Wiggly's are unacceptable for the expedition.

Every man should be trimmed with a high arch. Servants and the lowly (footmen, valets, puppy masters, tanners, dung stove tenders, penguin tamers, cooks) should all be outfitted with bowl cuts, the high and tight, or bowl cuts with balded pate, similar to the style of a Benedictine.

Officers benefit from the high and mighty, the brush top, the thorny canyon, or the wee folk run amok in the valley.

As for bearding, all men deemed capable may indulge

their selves in as much facial hair as they can muster. The overgrowth, the boot strap, the Amazonian, the chimney sweep, or the busker's broom are all acceptable styles.

The flavor saver, the pussy tickler, and the refined pussy tickler, the chevron, the magnum, along with the soup catcher should be considered acceptable expedition moustache styles.

Whatever style the gentleman chooses he must, by no means, make his gonads glabrous by shaving, scraping, waxing, or by any other means. The hair of the gonads may be trimmed, but no means be excessive about it. Gonadal hair is a lady's proof of manly vigor!

A variety of waxes and potions exist to assist the gentleman explorer in the upkeep of his hair. Mrs. Right A Way's Tincture of Opium Scalp and Gonad Restorer does a most admirable business of planting the seeds of a healthy bush wherever the drops may land. So does Lamb's Pussy Tickler Toner and Straightener.

A man must remember to not place acetone or lye on his nipples, for the resulting caustic burns and outrageous swelling could delay the expedition by a month or more.

In the selection of men for the expedition, see to it that they are supplied with ample portions of head, body, and facial hair, as this will give an indication of their overall vigor and manliness. Observe that brutes with hairy knuckles and thick, dark arm hair typically have a violent nature and a low IQ. These strapping specimens are built for manual labor.

Those with hairy palms, should be summarily dismissed from expedition duty, as this is a sign of excess self-abuse, and impending madness or idiocy.

The explorer should carry in his shaving kit: one katana, or samurai sword. This is used to trim the head, neck and body. No other implement need be used except a sharpened stone.

SELECTING THE RIGHT MEN FOR THE EXPEDITION

The selection of men is a crucial aspect of every expedition. If not chosen carefully, an expedition commander could be stuck with a bunch of lollygagging lay-abouts.

Physical appearance is the surest indicator of future performance on the expedition. White men may not always be the right men, as those lads with the pasty white skin of the stay-at-home may have never been tested against our enemy, Mother Nature. Choose instead lads whose swarthiness, creased brows and calloused man-hands show signs of physical labor and endless toil.

In order to select the best men for the expedition based

on physical traits, stand all candidates in a line naked
at attention. Squeeze each of their biceps as well as the
right and left buttock to test for firmness and strength of
purpose. As you squeeze each buttock, have your second in
command walk around the front of the line. If any of the
men rise to half or full staff during the aforenoted procedure, you may dismiss them as unfit for regular duty (however, they may qualify for assignment as expedition poof).
If, on the other hand, flaccidity is at all times maintained,
then fitness for duty may be surmised.

Additionally, each of the men's testes should be weighed
and measured to ensure the proper degree of manliness
can be maintained even under the most unforgiving conditions.

Next, observe that the feet are clean and clear of ulcer-
ations, abnormal bony prominences, and fungal infesta-
tions. Without a proper set of feet, a man may be tempted
to resort to the crampons.

After inspecting the feet, play a jaunty tune on the
gramophone and order the men to "make their pecs
dance." The dancing pectoral muscles should display uni-
lateral volitional movement in the frontal plane, as well as
highly developed bilateral coordination.

Upon verifying the soundness of each man's physical
structure, instruct each man to spit and to urinate as far
as he can, and carefully note your observations. Men who
can spit farther than urinate should be dismissed as unfit
for duty. Next, order the men to perform 75 butt kicks in
rapid succession, then observe the elasticity of each buttock. Finally, have each man bite down on a stick while

his partner attempts to remove it from his mouth. Time the results.

In additional to general physical traits, each man must be ideally suited to his particular expedition assignment. See to it that your radio man has large, protruding ears. The cook should have a curly mustache and an Italian or French accent. The expedition sculptor must have a chiseled jaw line. The porters should have the faces and tails of asses. The expedition poof must have limp wrists and a pronounced lisp. The navigator should have a head like a globe, a nose like a sextant, and a spinning, needle-like penis that always points north. The grenadier and machine-gunner should have mouths like howitzers, and speak in staccato, clipped sentences.

While these are the traits of the men, the traits of the leader are of capital importance. As commander you must have rank and title that befits your station. If you have a peerage, you must order the men to refer to you with the honorific of your title, whether that be "sir" or "duke," and etcetera. If you have no peerage, you must claim an appropriate title such as Colonel, Centurion, Imperator, or Tsar.

Your gonads should be twice the weight of the next man's stones. They must leave a distinct pattern as they trail through the dirt betwixt your solid, oaken legs. You must stand always with your feet as far apart as possible, hands on hips or waving in the air. When you speak, your whisper should be louder than the next loudest man's shout. Your gesticulations should be sweeping and dramatic when addressing the men. You should stare into the eyes of each man until he lowers his gaze respectfully.

Each step you take should shake the ground beneath you. When not engaged in other purposeful activity, your hands should be balled into fists, always ready to strike at the first sign of adversity or insubordination. Your aggressive, dominant stance will be of the greatest comfort to the men. Occasionally, for a bit of sport you may wish to playfully knock a man out and kick him as he lies in the dirt. This will show you to be the magnanimous father-figure that the lads will look up to you as.

MOUNTAIN MAN PSYCHOLOGY: Bag Up Your Troubles and Bring `Em Up the Mountain

The mountain is an evil place, overseen by wicked gods whose malevolent intent is written in the many deathtraps waiting to ensnare unwary mortals. The intensity of this evil is such that it reaches a kind of purity of essence, a kind of sickening beauty to behold. Because of this purity, the mountain is the best natural therapist on the planet. The mountain is a silent judge, an indifferent listener. It invites you to bring all of your psychological baggage and unwrap it, revealing it to the mountain gods like a dirty diaper.

The best method of unfolding this disposable, be-smirched undergarment, is to go on several climbs with your mountaineering partner, silently taking note of any weaknesses or bad habits you may perceive on each climb. Write these down in a notebook in order to maintain an accurate record. Be sure to note even seemingly minor weaknesses such as "partner looks winded" or "too slow." This will help you provide a thorough assessment of their faults when the right opportunity presents itself. And when is the right time to bring your climbing partner's attention to their faults and weaknesses? At camp? While planning the next trip? During a quiet lull in the climbing?

No, no and no! Times and places like those noted above do not allow for the proper release of tension, or for a true or fair discussion of the problems at hand.

Preferably, all of the following conditions should be met before you begin discussing interpersonal differences:

1. You must be at or above 10,671 feet. It is only in the crisp, thin air of high elevation that manly differences can be sorted out. At lower elevations, the reasoning centers of the brain are slow to form logical conclusions, whereas at high altitude thoughts become as clear as the air itself

2. Your discussion of differences should proceed more like a lecture, diatribe or interrogation. Attack first, and hit below the belt. Be sure to bring up irrelevant facts that have no bearing on the situation. If this fails to obtain a result, try shame, insults, ad hominem

attack or humiliation.

3. Whatever happens, never back down. Do you want to be the alpha dog? Then stick to your guns and keep firing without pausing to reload.

4. If words don't work, try fists. Or at least use threatening or intimidating gestures to get your point across. Draw your katana, and wave it around. This will let him know who the boss is.

5. If all else fails, brain your partner with the blunt side of the axe. By not heeding your rules, your partner has rightfully earned his one-way ticket to beat-down street. This won't kill him, and will likely only cause a minor concussion. If you see blood coming out of the ears or eyes, or if the pupils of his eyes become fixed and dilated—hit a little more softly. Once the melee is finished, wait until the ringing has subsided in your partner's ears before moving on, as this will enhance his ability to obey your verbal commands.

**SAMPLE DIALOGUE
SCENARIO:**

Sir Edmund Cornforth: Look here, you've been mucking about with your hands in your trousers this whole trip. You've been weeping like a little girl.

Sir Randall Ponce Fanny: What's your problem mate? Been tugging your wire a little too long then?

Sir Edmund Cornforth: All I'm saying is that you'd best pull up your britches and take your thumb out of your arse. I say it for your own good. You've done nothing this entire trip but gasp for air like a bloody goldfish on land. No need to be a wanker about it.

Sir Randall Ponce Fanny: Piss off then. I have not.

Sir Edmund Cornforth: I really think you should phone that tart you were making eyes with at the ale house, you know, the one with the fishnets and herpes sores? I think she could arrange for emergency transport to wankerville. I hear it's quite nice there, this time of year.

Sir Randall Ponce Fanny: Sod you, you sick bastard.

Sir Edmund Cornforth: Oi! What was that then? A complaint from the public school leftenant? Out with it then, fanny boy.

Sir Randall Ponce Fanny: I'm warning you. Sod off mate.

Sir Edmund Cornforth: Oi! A threat? Is that what that was?

Sir Randall Ponce Fanny: No mate…look, let's just bury the axe until we get off the bloody mountain. It doesn't bode for us to be at each other's throats out here.

Sir Edmund Cornforth: You want to bury the axe? Well, I know just where to bury it! [pulls out axe and beats Sir Fanny with the blunt end]

HOW TO COMPORT ONE'S SELF
IN THE PRESENCE
OF OTHER HUMAN BEINGS

Now that you know how to comport yourself around the other members of your party, you must now learn the appropriate method of conduct around other human beings. Expedition members should not be confused with human beings.

Mountains, while forbidding, remote places, are often not as solitary as one would think or prefer. The world is a large place, but one that can be difficult to share with others. Therefore, gentlemen must have rules by which they can abide whenever encountering each other—often in competition for fame and Glory—whilst occupying the same mountain.

On Settling Disputes

Whenever a descending party meets an ascending party on a narrow trail, the ascending party must wave a red flag as the signal of "fair warning" before creating a gap using sharp shoulders and rough elbows.

A line in the snow should be drawn around your camp, so that any who encroach on the camp space without permission may fairly meet with severe corporal punishment. A member of the party should stand guard at all hours with a drawn katana to enforce this edict. Mark the boundaries of your camp or your territory with a stream of urine. Add a fresh stream of urine to the boundary every two hours until every man has exhausted his urinary output. Each man should drink four cups of tea every hour to aid this purpose, but not so much tea that it places undue strain upon his kidneys.

As a courtesy to those who may be sick, injured, lost, or in need of help—use only a bamboo cane to enforce rule #2 if any of the above conditions are met, thereby minimizing pain and distress while still maintaining the honor and integrity of the expedition.

When two parties make a claim on a limited resource simultaneously, a line should be drawn in the snow, across which the two strongest men of either party fight until death or dismemberment using no weapons. If a standoff is reached, then each party must select a dueling captain to resolve the dispute. The selection must be made by means of drawing straws (a straw drawing kit and a back-up straw drawing kit should be packed in the porters' saddle bags).

The dueling captains of either party must follow standard dueling procedure, with the only difference being that the required number of paces should be foreshortened due to scarce level ground. The duel must be fought to the death, with no quarter asked, and no quarter granted. If, upon firing, each dueling captain kills the other simultaneously, no victor can be declared, and a second set of dueling captains must be elected and the process repeated until a clear victor emerges.

If however, every member of each party happens to be killed during the execution of this process—leaving only one man alive from each party, then each man may exercise the option to fight to the death or shake hands and forgive the insult, as their individual temperaments allow. With either option, the requirements of honor are met.

If two parties reach the summit of the mountain simultaneously, they should each plant their respective flags. The party with the longest flagpole (and thus the higher flag) is deemed to have summited first. Girth of the flagpole is not as significant as overall length. A bifurcated or trifurcated flagpole is considered more acceptable than a single-pointed pole. It is therefore incumbent upon each expedition to plan accordingly, and carry extra lengths of flagpole in case this—all too common—situation arises.

Gentlemen are honor-bound to render aid and assistance to any personage they find to be ill, injured, lost or in need of help. A gentleman must first proceed by ascertaining the type of assistance required.

PROCEDURES FOR RENDERING AID AND ASSISTANCE

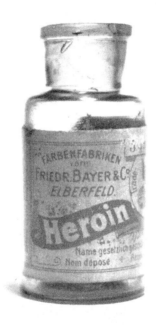

After identifying a potential aid recipient and verifying their peaceful intensions (be wary of yeti primate trickery), shout: "state the type of assistance you require!" Do not render aid until the injured person gives the requisite three signal blasts from their assistance horn (two short and one long) and then yells, "I say, assistance needed here my good man!"

If the person is lost, explain to how to make a "mental map" as outlined in a later chapter.

If the person is hungry, offer to explain how hunger pangs are merely a temporary bout of unmanliness which are sure to pass.

If the person is thirsty, roll snow into a large snowball, and roll the snowball to the dehydration victim. If snow is not available, use balls of frozen man-urine. Never imbibe the urine of an ass or pack-mule.

If the person has taken ill, or shows symptoms of debility offer them two teaspoons of Mrs. Right-A-Way's Tincture of Opium Cure-All.

If the person has a broken bone, extend the infirm limb, then bind the proximal and distal joints tightly using hemp cord.

If the person is bleeding, sprinkle the wound with Mrs. Right-A-Way's Tincture of Witch Hazel Cure-All, and pack the wound with clean sawdust.

Burns should be sealed using yak or yeti butter.

Mountain madness or fits of raving should be cured with a solid, back-handed slap to the face.

Yeti bites, while painful, are seldom deadly. Use a yeti-bite kit to make an incision around the wound, and suck out the poison, spitting out the poisoned blood with each mouthful. Then find the offending beast and swipe of its head with the katana, and kick it down the mountain.

Piles—the "gentleman's bane" should be treated by packing the anus with dry gunpowder and sand at a ratio of 1:1. A diet rich in hard tack will quickly ameliorate this disease.

Failure to thrive or general malaise are psychological in nature, and can only be remedied by vigorous exercise, and full body exposure to clean, crisp air.

HOW TO PERFORM AN EMERGENCY HORIZONTAL BRO HUG

The bro hug is a dangerous and complex maneuver that carries risks even in its simpler, vertical form. If it is performed for even one second too long, it can boil over into mollycoddling or worse, it can turn both the hugger and the hugee gay. The vertical bro hug allows for weight-shifting away from the center of the bro, and the operation of normal survival reflexes that naturally tend to repulse physical affection between men.

The emergency horizontal bro hug (EHBH) should only be attempted in the direst of situations, only when the hugee is unable to safely stand erect. The EHBH should only be deployed when a solid, back-handed slap would not provide greater comfort, when the hugee has only a few hours to live, when their steely resolve has failed, and only when both parties are manly enough that the risk of gayness to each is acceptably minimal.

The EHBH can never be performed when the hugee is lying in the prone position with his bum facing the hugger, as this position could turn them both gay.

A gaydar should be used in order to detect dangerous levels of gayness that may arise from unhealthy levels of male-to-male physical contact. Because gaydars come in many different varieties, be sure that you are familiar with its use and operation before attempting to deploy it in field situations. If the gaydar beeps or detects dangerous levels of gayness, immediately disengage from the bro hug and retreat from the gay zone.

If the hugee is found by the hugger in the prone position, the hugger should roll the hugee into a supine position. The hugee should cross his legs at the ankles and clench his thighs around his crotch. This will protect the hugger from any potential gayness that may escape from the hugee's genitals.

Next, the hugger should place his dominant knee on the lateral aspect of the hugee's knee of choice. The hugger should, at this point, don a thick, kevlar vest which will protect both parties from any gay molecules that may have escaped into the ether.

Upon donning the vest, the hugger should bend his knee and shift his weight so that his dominant shoulder touches the proximate shoulder of the hugee. The hugger should turn his head away from the face of the hugee to ensure that cheek-to-cheek contact does not occur. Then, the hugger should retreat immediately from this stance and place a hand of choice onto the hugee's proximal shoulder and give three solid squeezes and shakes deploying a vice-like grip.

At this moment, place the hugee at ease with the use of a comforting phrase such as, "very good then, very good! Once more into the breach old bean!" Or you may say, "Stiff upper lip, but nothing else stiff old boy!" Or you may say, "Don't worry lad, this is not gay at all!" Terminate the physical contact with a cough, and an awkward shuffling of feet.

HOW TO TERMINATE A FELLOW CREATURE'S SUFFERING WITH A MINIMUM OF FUSS

If a gentleman explorer encounters another person or party who appear to be near death, he is honor-bound to ease their suffering and procure for them a proper burial. Easing of suffering can take place in one of two ways. First, if ammunition stores allow, one may dispatch the victim with one shot to the head at point-blank range. Exercise this option at least 5 meters from drinking water sources. Use of a .40 calibre weapon or higher is recommended in order to be sure of instantaneously collapsing of the brain pan.

Secondly, if this is not practicable, you can offer the victim three tablespoons of Mrs.Right–A–Way's Tincture of Opium Cure All. If, after imbibing three tablespoons of Mrs. Right–A–Way's Tincture of Opium Cure All and a shot to the head fail to achieve the desired effect, then bury the victim in snow, making him as comfortable as possible.

Remember, several (no more than three) pats on the shoulder and a stiff salute are acceptable comfort measures, but absolutely NO MOLLYCODDLING. The Emergency Horizontal Bro Hug is allowed, but under no circumstances can more than two points of contact occur, or else it shall turn you gay.

After this entire process has been completed, some effort should be expended in order to determine the victim's wishes relevant to the best manner of ending their suffering, as well as a mailing address and the names of next-of-kin. Once the person is dead, give them a "snow burial," wrap them in a sleeping bag, and remove none of their personal effects except for their leather bound, acid-resistant adventure journal and personal identification papers.

If the dying man can conjure no final words as best befits the profundity of his impending demise recommend that he choose from one of the following statements for final, last words, or refer to *Dr. Browntrout's Unabridged Guide to Suggested Last Words and Final Statements For the Doomed, the Damned and the Dying*:

Father...always did know best.

Meow love you_____
(insert name of wife/delete name of mistress here)
Look after meow kee-kees.

I go to death a free man, for glory I hath seized!

I'm terribly sorry for the mess. Here, put a bit of petrol on
me and I will clasp my trembling fingers round my last match
and thus spare you the energy expenditure of my burial.
Do cover your noses till it is done.

Cruel fate, I hate thee not! These hands hath tried thee, and
these hands hath failed. But try, try they did,
and I be a better man for the effort.

Give my last tin of Spotted Dick to the lads.
You may wish to pour a bit of grog in it,
for the tuning fork rings against it harder than a yeti egg.

In death I say:
woe to you, woe to you all who have not lived.

To Queen I surrender the glory, to Country,
my life, to the tax man, my wallet.
I lament that I can but give no more than that.

Mrs. Right—A—Way, you've a voice like an angel.
You speak to me in dreams.

Mummy, I say I've been a naughty lad.
Forgive me, mum, and do tuck me in this one last time.
I'll not hide the biscuits in the sheets again, I promise.

Wrap me in the Union Jack, lads,

but do cut out small holes for my eyes and my mouth.
That way, I cannot fail to inspire you.
Do smite these heedless heathens with
a headlong, heavy hammer.

Damn you death! Damn you to hell!

Lament not these lamentations,
for they shall not lament for thee.

Gentlemen I'm afraid I must confess, I am the Lizard King.

———◆———

Here are a list of…er…um…well, shall we say awkward statements that you should pretend not to hear, should you hear them. Do the dying man a kind turn by turning away and coughing into your hand like this: "Ah, ah-hem! I say, uh, ah-hem! What was that? Sorry old face, I completely lost you there."

Mummy, I wet myself again. Do put away the bristle brush. I'll be a good boy next time.

God forgive me, spotted dick isn't the only kind I like.

Dear belly, please make me a unicorn in the next life. A rainbow unicorn, with glitter and faery tinsel.

Hitch me to a post lads and give me fresh straw.

I am a centaur, but my hind legs are invisible.

Marybelle, which one is she?
Is that my wife or is she...my other wife?

I know that little Trevor and Ian aren't mine.
You tell that red-headed lorry driver
that I know what else he's been driving.

I've...I've been so naughty. Please, put the cuffs on and spank
me like the saucy, misbehaving gentleman explorer I am.

Leave my body here in this frozen grave,
but do bring my manhood home in a jar.
Give it to whichever one my wife is.

I love all you lads like brothers. Here, give me a full-contact
bear hug and kiss my cheeks like the Italians do.

I'm sorry lads, I'm afraid I'm no Highlander, and this isn't
a tartan underneath me. It's just a plaid skirt.

French wine...is better than British ale.

God save the Queen...the fascist regime.

Bollocks to you, mountain! And bollocks to this
damned expedition! And bollocks to all of you sods!

Oh dear me, my liver is pickled.

Do preserve it for medical science, old thing.

Please lads, help me change out of
these lacey women's underdrawers...
though they were always the most comfortable.

Don't tell my wife that my first time was with
Rory Rotten Crotch.

ALPINE ADVENTURE PLANNING:
Planning Is For The Weak

Many explorers spend months or even years planning their expedition with meticulous precision. They study multiple routes. They familiarize themselves with technical climbing techniques, using ropes, harnesses, straps, chains and pulleys. These people are feeble minded, and you should never listen to them. While they hang out at camping supply retailers shining their crampons and flirting with the cashiers, you'll be three-quarters of the way to death and halfway to Glory!

Life—and death—are spontaneous adventures that require no planning and betoken no preparation. John Lennon once said, "life is what happens while you're making plans." Wise words, considering he was a hippie. Death may be waiting for you around any corner, at any time. Do you want to die at your desk or on the side of mountain? Death will choose you at the appointed time, and you will have no chance to bargain your way out of it with a bunch of sissy-ass planning. We cannot choose the hour and manner of our deaths, but we can choose to die ringed by wreaths of Glory. But unlike death, Glory will not ride out to meet you on the plain of strife. If you want Glory, you must hunt it down, seize it and tackle it to the ground, and beat it to death, never letting go for an instant until it has been subdued like a wild animal.

Here is a list of everything you will need to seize glory from the summit:

High def video camera (or other action cam)—
with space for hours of footage and days of battery life.

In the days of yore, the glorybound told their tales round a huge oak table, whilst slamming down chrome-plated tankards of ale and regaling the people with songs of their deeds. Nowadays, you must be ready to upload your expedition pictures to "the facebook" the moment they are taken. Your digital media capture device is the single-most important tool of the trip.

Katana (samurai sword)—this venerable weapon is versatile, and looks totally badass when you swing it around whilst traversing glaciers and snowfields. Combined with black pants and face-mask, you can be ready to take the mountain by stealthy means—as some serious mountain Ninjas have already done.

Double-headed battle axe—the very fact of the extra weight and inconvenience of carrying such a weapon make it a suitable prop for your glory-seeking quest. A chrome or polished steel axe will cost a little extra, but it will look amazing as the sun glints off of it as you raise it over your head at the summit. Pick up one of these, and leave the ice-axes for the yuppies at yuppie high-end sporting gear retail store, not otherwise specified.

.44 pistol—do you really need one of these? Yes, because mountain goats are too fast to hack at with a sword, and let's face it: goat meat tastes great. And even if you don't see a goat, there will surely be smaller and more defense-less creatures ambling about; some of them may even show a striking innocence with regard to the presence of man. If this occasion should come to pass, or you feel bored and want to take pot shots at the rocks, you'll wish you never left home without your .44 and an extra box of hollowpoint rounds.

Shoe spikes—if you feel you must diminish your share of glory by utilizing equipment that artificially extends your life, then at least do not bring equipment that diminishes your manhood in the process. Men of honor do not wear or speak of "crampons." In certain situations, where death appears likely to come too far ahead of Glory, some honorable men choose to don shoe spikes—but never, ever crampons. It hardly needs to be spelled out why.

A leather-bound, paper journal—this is NOT to be confused with a diary or other means to record weakness (see the chapter on adventure writing). This is a backup, glory-recording device. Honorable gentlemen record their hardships, and the stoic manner with which they shouldered their burdens in a logical, linear, chronological format. Do not engage in unmanly forms of narrative like experimental writing. Real men are straightforward and follow literary conventions! The purpose of the journal is to provision you with posthumous Glory, should it be found upon your mummified corpse at the bottom of a crevasse or lying supine, flexed in climbing position at the bottom of a forbidding talus slope. When the elements have destroyed your action camera and the high def is gone and the cracked lens can no longer be your eye, and your manly voice is stilled forever—choose your words carefully and let your journal tell the tale of your struggle.

A sheepskin jacket and a scruffy, wooly beard—these are tools that will let your audience know that you are totally serious about the mountain-climbing thing.

Here are the items that a gentleman never takes on an expedition in descending order of their violation of honor:

Supplemental oxygen—this is the worst device that any man can carry. You may as well cut off your own testicles before you begin if you think Glory will be won with the use of supplemental oxygen. Gentlemen breathe whatever air they encounter, whether that be ground air, or hydrogen sulfide belched out of volcanic vents. Real men do not wince at the idea of inhaling a bit of thin, crisp air now and then. It adds vigor to the spirit! So what if your tea takes a little longer to boil. Suck it up. Don't cry about it.

GPS, smartphones, mountain rescue locator unit, map or compass—use of these items will rob you of all honor. A man who cannot find his way up a mountain without the use of a satellite is no man at all. A man who needs a pocket compass has no moral compass. A man who reads a map is not reading the snow and ice, the clouds or the rocks. Techno-gadgets provide a false sense of security and interfere with your relationship with the mountain. Smartphones can only bring honor when they are used to upload your pictures of being crowned in wreaths of Glory Laurels on facebook. The only honorable way to send any signal on a mountain is to fire flare guns and signal rockets when it appears that death is imminent and you need a party to retrieve your corpse and crown it with honors.

First aid kit—there is nothing more dishonorable than tending to an injury rather than manning up and soldiering on. Is nothing sacred anymore? Pain is the price of victory! Blood is the currency of the brave! If you must bring any medicines, follow Teddy Roosevelt's method: bring only one, lethal dose of morphine (or a jug of Mrs. Right A Way's Tincture of Opium Cure-All) so as to avoid being a burden to anyone in the party if you become lamed by a fall or illness. Bandages are the scarlet letter of the weak. Don't allow crutches to be your crutch. Splints are things you remove with tweezers, not something to be worn with pride. Eschew these trappings of survival.

Ski poles, ice axe, ropes, belts, chains, carabiners, harnesses—these items were not intended or designed to bestow honor, but to artificially prolong your life. Manly strength, brute force, unflagging endurance, and willpower are the best tools of the gentleman mountaineer. Never allow them to rust, or you will fail. If anything, you should carry sandbags around your neck and ankles in order to prolong the depth of your manly self-punishment.

Protein powders, energy drinks, pills, dope or energy bars—real men rely only on the fat reserves they carry around their midriff. If those inner reserves are not sufficient to carry them through, then they must perish. Nothing is more abhorrent than using speed, protein, lipids, carbohydrates or other kinds of dope in order to keep going. Willpower does not come from a bottle. Bravery cannot be found in a vitamin-enriched bar. Strength of character contains no guarine, caffeine or any other –eine! Only dope-heads do dope. Meat, penguin milk, hard tack and rum alone are enough for a man.

BUILDING STRENGTH:
Strength is for the strong

If you are weak, you will never be strong. We all started out as babies, but if you look at a baby very carefully, you will see that some babies are strong, iron-willed and iron-fisted while others are pudgy weaklings. Baby eagles push each other out of the nest in order to prove their strength to the mother. Baby sharks eat one another in the mother shark's womb. Humans don't really do that, because we're better than that. Never the less, the point remains the same: only the strong are destined to thrive and only the weak are destined to be eaten.

How do you know if you're strong? Take off all of your clothes and look in the mirror. Are you able to put down your arms? Yes? Then you are weak. Do you have a lot of chest hair? This is a sign that you have an abundance of vital force energy.

Another proven measure of strength is the length and

girth of your penis. Two inches wide by eight inches long while flaccid is the minimum requirement. You can measure your penis with measuring tape, but do not artificially stretch or pull your member because that's cheating. The circumference of your gonads is also an excellent measure of your strength and integrity. The gonads should be proportionally spherical, not oblong or conical. The right and left testicles should be the same size and shape, and should symmetrically swing together in lock step as a single, disciplined unit within the scrotal sac.

This symmetry is more important than the weight and the circumference of the gonads, as is commonly believed. None the less, you should weigh and measure your gonads for additional indicators of your strength, vital force energy and overall manliness. Average ball weight should amount to no less than 5 lbs. per teste. This simple equation should assist you in the aforenoted endeavor.

Total Scrotal Sac Weight (TSSW) (right testicle + left testicle)	**X**	Total Hair Covered Body Surface (THCBS)	**=**	Manliness

In order to determine your total scrotal sac weight (TSSW), place your scrotal sac on an industrial scrotometer, and adjust the aspect-ratio settings to determine the estimated girth of each gonad separately.

By using these standardized measurements, you will be

able to determine the eigenvalues of each teste after a simple regression analysis using varimax rotation. Estimating total hair-covered body surface is a little more dicey; you will need a three-sided mirror, a video camera and a hand-held mirror in order to perform an accurate survey of the anal and perianal regions.

Once the survey is completed, you can utilize hair Thubenhoffer's Micro-Flora Thickness Testing to determine the density of the surface flora of your body.

The gonads are incredibly important. Inside each gonad is a miniature factory that pumps out testosterone day and night. Testosterone puts hair on your chest, and fire in your belly. It creates tiny animalcules that journey into a woman's birth canal in order to seek and conquer an egg. This is the seed. This is where it all begins. Every man, woman and child began as an animalcule—a tiny swimmer—in the gonad of a man. Sperm is the grapeshot and cannonade to be fired from your man howitzer to rain down on waiting woman's eggs like bombs!

Without testosterone, our species would succumb to apathy and slackerism. Testosterone is what made the cave men want to jab a crude spear-point into the belly of a wooly mammoth. Use the following chart as a "quick and dirty" chart to determine manliness. The vertical axis is the total scrotal sac weight (TSW) and the horizontal axis is the length of the penile shaft. The combination of these values is reported in manliness units (MU).

PLEASE REFER TO THE SCALE BELOW TO INTERPRET YOUR RESULTS.

Manliness Units (MU)

Rating 0-3

MWBV (man with breasts and vagina)

Rating 4-5

MWV (man with vagina)

Rating 6-7

Nub-like Penis (trace)

Rating 8-9

Mid-range Penis

Rating 10-11

NMG (Normal Masculine Gonads)

Rating 11-11.5

EMG (Enlarged Masculine Gonads)

Rating 11.6+

HTMG (Hypertrophic Masculine Gonads)

Once your calculations are completed, you will have an objective and accurate measure of your relative strength and manliness ranging from weak-ass, limp-dick, boyman to badass, steel crushing, steroid monster.

Speaking of the gonads, it hardly needs to be mentioned, but real men never, ever masturbate. Only a weakling would not be able to find a woman to initiate the release of the man seed. Animals such as monkeys masturbate; because of their sick and depraved natures, they don't know any better. We laugh and point at their silly antics, but with humans it's far more serious. Masturbation causes insanity, blindness and iron deficiency—and that's the worst of all. Without iron, a man has nothing. Chronic masturbators loose feeling in the tips of their fingers, causing a loss of gross and fine motor coordination. Masturbation can also lead to intension tremors, excess sweaty palms, and fear of the dark. Masturbation is immoral, because it deprives a woman of her claim to your seed. No masturbator has ever climbed a mountain.

BUILDING CHARACTER: Character Can't Be Built.

IT IS FORGED IN A BATH OF STEELY RESOLVE

You can build a house, but you cannot "build" the master of the house. You can build a truck, but you cannot "build" a truck driver. You can build a bird house, but you cannot "build" a bird. You can build a trail, but you cannot "build" a hiker. You cannot build a man. You can grow a man. You cannot build character. Character is forged, not built. How is character forged? It is forged in a bath of steely resolve.

Steely resolve is the determination to win at all costs, no matter what the price. It's crushing your enemies until they're completely smooshed.

Do you want that mountain? Then go out and take it, bite off a piece of it. Spit out the piece. Bite off another piece. Spit that piece out, until the entire mountain is nothing but pea-sized rubble. Are you going to whine because you might lose a few teeth in the process, or are you going to spit out the blood and your teeth, and keep biting with whatever you have left? That is steely resolve.

Forging character necessitates the destruction of the body, yours and others who stand in your way. Accept no substitute. Allow no compromise. If a wild panda bear bites off your arm, spray blood in its face from your spurting stump and use the bitten arm like a club with your other arm to beat it into submission! If a panda bear bites off both of your arms, lie on your back and use your feet to kick the beast to death. If a panda bear bites off both of your arms and one leg, that still leaves one good leg you can use as a weapon to smite your furry enemy. That is character. That is resolve. That is determination. That is class.

MASTERING YOUR FEAR:
You are Either Born Brave or Die a Coward

Fear is nothing more than the body's way of testing you to see if you are a coward. Only the weak fear fear. Real men laugh at fear, spit on fear, and crush it beneath the boot heel of their steely resolve. Some people confuse adrenaline with fear. Adrenaline is part of the kick-ass nervous system. Certain types of endolphins begin to pump vigorously through your chest wall, and into the heart muscle. These endolphins propel you to fight, to conquer, to perform feats of great strength. It is the ringing in your ears and the pounding of your heart as you behead a yeti with your axe. That is not fear: it's just your neurogenic endolphin kick-ass response (NEKAR).

Real fear emanates from doubt, and only milksops doubt. Real men know their mission and their purpose. You have come to the mountain to climb it, not to "find yourself" or to figure out if it should be climbed.

Never question anything you set out to do and you will be guided like a bullet down the rifle barrel of your steely resolve and be launched like a ballistic missile with your strength of purpose. Start to doubt any of that, and it's game over, baby.

Your brain is the scope of the rifle and your body is the bullet. Fear is the bullet-proof body-armor worn by the mountain to prevent you from penetrating it. Only you can make the choice to piss on the grave of fear, and kick over its tombstone.

The coward is a man without mastery. He gets his ideas out of fancy books that tell him to worry about everything. He takes no action, but dithers over every decision. He consults numerous, flaccid advisors and counselors who do nothing but jerk him off and validate his self-esteem. He is a nothing, a nobody, a zero.

MANAGING AFFAIRS OF THE HOMEFRONT

It so happens that many expeditions take place over the course of months, years or decades. Sadly most gentlemen explorers are faced with the prospect of having to leave behind a loving wife, a nanny, a governess, a wet nurse, scullery maids, a disgraced, drunken elder brother, foot men, a concierge, housekeepers, a tea waiter, the dinner staff, the chamber maids, the chamber pots, the parlor maids, the game keeper, the charwoman, the fencing tutor, dowdy in-laws, the livery boys, the mustachio maintenance technician, the gardeners, the sous chef, the head chef, the songsmiths and balladeers, the milk maid, the foxing hounds, the valets, the riding stallions, the racing stallions, the house grammarian, the cobbler, haberdasher, the lambs and ewelets, the hutch bunnies, and the hutch mites that inhabit the inhabitants of the hutches.

And also the gentleman's brood: his spawn, the fruits of his loins, a.k.a. "children."

It is best that the loving father instill his authority from an early age, insisting that his children refer to him as Colonel, Leftenant, or sir. A father, in turn should refer to his children only by Mr. or Ms. combined with last name. This is an excellent way of cutting out extra mollycoddling than can weaken a child's natural agression and will to survive.

It is quite natural that the explorer's children should fear and love their father in equal measure. You can instill love by taking the boys on safari in Africa before leaving on your adventure. Make sure that the lads get a kill no matter how long the odds. Until the boys have killed, they cannot call themselves men. As for the girls, buy them mother-of-pearl combs and other useless baubles in order to secure their respect. If yours is a pretty but petulant young lass who is difficult to please, buy her a pony and name it Strawberry. Inform the girl that if she is not right and good while you are gone, Strawberry will be killed and fed to the yeti. If such an unfortunate state of events comes to pass, explain to your daughter, "Strawberry is now an angel who frolics in Pony Heaven, a much, much less cruel place than a yeti cave. Dry your tears, girl child.

You will thank me later."

No loving relationship is possible without fear. The mollycoddled lad grows to become the milksop man. Corporal punishment is both kind and stern correction that builds moral character, and instills an immediate love of discipline and authority, especially so with the wayward youth. Therefore, beat your spawn at regular intervals. Use a switch, a rod, cudgel, cane, or a heavy, leaded pipe. Rap the knuckles, smack the bare bottom, box their ears, or brain them if they attempt to run.

Remember, a good father never hits out of anger, but only with love—even when he is enraged. A father's love of his children always takes the form of rigid, militaristic discipline. It is best to issue sound thumpings only when the child least expects it. For instance, after lovingly reading a bedtime story, hide in your child's closet with a stick. Then, when they are asleep, leap out of the closet, and wave the stick in the air and shout, "damn you, damn you, damn you!" If the child fails to cry, thump them once. Then thump them again once they do begin crying. Then, explain that, "father only does this because he loves you. You will thank me for it later."

Or better yet, offer your child a toy bear with a ticking clock stuffed inside. Explain that "Spreckles" the bear is very angry, and has a bomb inside his tummy. Speckles loves daddy, and will watch over and take notes on everything the children do whilst daddy is away in the Himalaya, and if they're bad, his stomach will explode, killing everyone and sending them to hell.

Sometimes it so happens that children will pick up filthy

habits while their father's influence wanes. Often, while father is away in the Himalaya, his physical presence at home is limited to a portrait on the mantelpiece of him scowling and raising a large cudgel. Left under the wing of a weak and puny mother, children are apt to turn into feral creatures void of morals. If such ragamuffinry overtakes your brood, you must act quickly.

Sometimes boys of a certain age begin to be tempted by Satan to stimulate their gonads. Often this is done in secret, but sometimes an errant lad will be caught in the act. Other times, a boy is found out because he presents with sweaty palms, shifty eyes, or his eyesight begins to dim. This is a serious matter, as wanton self-abuse has turned many a lad with a bright future into a drooling idiot suitable only for the lunatic asylum. Worse, it can turn a lad into a sodomite.

Should this nefarious state of events come to pass, instruct your drunken, elder brother to box the lad's ears until they fairly hum with the vengeance of the Lord. Then have him taken to a sweaty, lonely priest to confess his sins. If this fails to cure the problem, saltwater baths with ample portions of cayenne pepper should rectify the situation. If not, then a chastity belt and mitten-handed gloves should prevent future attempts. While your drunken brother may have to wear out many oaken cudgels braining the young fornicator, steady perseverance always brings about cure!

While the lads may be in need of more correction, the lasses are no less worrisome. While father is gone, they often become the subject of inquiry by randy lads seeking to escort them to the debutante ball. Of course, this is patently unacceptable, as a father must subject potential suitors to a full and thorough review before allowing any such uncouth lad to bask in their daughter's virginal glow.

While many lads mean no harm, others are downright devious, propelled by poisonous gonads to seek more than your daughter's hand. Some of these lads have even perpetuated the myth that a young maiden may yet keep her innocence if she but consents to the popping of her "anal cherry," and parts not her maiden fern. Therefore, before he leaves, a good father must instill a dose of bitter medicine in his daughter to inoculate against her against such amoral attempts at amorousness.

Take the girl aside and speak to her thus: "Good daughter, protect your back door as well as the front, for there is an enemy at the gates. He would storm your castle by any means he can find. Once the gate comes down, your palace is overcome, and your kingdom, lost. Do remember your kegels, and clench tightly, for poisonous gonads lurk in the night, just beyond your walls. Only the staunchest defense may prevent them from kidnapping you and turning your temple of purity into a house of ill repute."

"This fiend who seeks you, brooks no reason. He seeks admittance in order to access your eggs, like a fox in the henhouse. He comes to you with a flesh spear, glistening with desperation. He would place his quivering love harpoon in any entrance to your scared garden he can find. Listen to me, young girl! Let him not engage your cherry in idle converse, for he would win your honor by trickery and other devilish means, and once he has it, he would besmirch it with all manner of sensuous proddings of the flesh. He would say 'I love you' a thousand times, for just one chance to produce perfidious ripples in your placid pond. Remember girl, your booty is Satan's bounty."

By liberally spraying your daughter and her suitors with a heavy dose of the revolting but effective First Kiss Piss Mist for the Young Miss—another revolutionary invention from that purveyor of good sense, Mrs. Right–A–Way—you may stave off some of the unwanted attentions of the lads.

If you suspect that your daughter cannot be trusted to safeguard her innocence while you are away, you must lock her in the upper floors of your estate along with your deformed or misshapen idiot children whose family shame you hide by keeping them out of sight.

If a girl should happen to be "spoiled," she should be disowned and deposited in the nearest gutter.

While the children of the gentleman explorer present their own complications, the wife of the explorer also presents difficulties. Remember your poor wife while you are gone, for your absence is a heavy cross that she must bear. Without your presence, your magnanimous, guiding light, she is unable to think for herself, to process information, or to make even the simplest decisions. You must, if necessary, leave her to the care of your drunken elder brother. Make sure that the family doctor gives her a liberal dose of Mrs. Right–A–Way's Tincture of Opium Cure all nightly. This will keep her disordered mind from fearful ruminations.

When not engaging female guests or adjusting her toilette, the explorer's wife should be pining for the explorer's loving, intrepid, intimidatingly manly presence at all times. She should be lying supine for at least 22 hours per day, with one, delicate, pasty arm draped limply over her face whilst issuing forth piteous sighs and doleful lamentations. In her other hand, she should be clutching a locket with your daguerreotype depicting you standing atop a dead American bison wielding a saber and an Enfield rifle.

Never should the explorer's wife dress or bathe herself, but she should be attended to by maids who will ensure that her milky fingers are never raised to perform even the lightest labors. She should not trouble her mind with books, artwork, or thoughts that would cloud her mind or poison her uterus with stirrings of hysteria. She should speak but little, faint often, and she should never attempt to vote. Any deviation from these prescribed womanly behaviors constitutes the worst betrayal a husband can experience, and they could lead to scandal, the madhouse, or worse.

ENCOUNTERS WITH THE YETI

Is the yeti a beast from hell, an innocent but troublesome primate, or a vanished species of subhuman, homo yeticus? Scientists are still attempting to resolve the mysteries of the enigmatic yeti (also called the abominable snowman or sasquatch). One thing is for sure, every mountaineer knows that if you spent enough time at the poles or above tree line, you are bound to encounter this majestic manimal.

From titillating speculation, we move to fact. Dead yeti specimens have revealed anthropometry studies that clearly demonstrate an average height for a sexually mature male at 9 feet tall, a well-developed thoracic cavity, and strongly opposable thumbs with the crushing force of an intensely crushing thing. Further, inch-long canines point to a predominantly carnivorous diet of strong mountain sheep.

Phrenologically speaking, this beast displays homicidal rage along with the simple mind of the morally corrupt. He is utterly devoid of right thinking or higher impulses. The food and copulation centers of the brain are swollen like circus balloons, whilst the centers for art, religion, temperance, and chastity are undeveloped, desert valleys deeper than an ocean trench.

This creature is no scavenger, but a hunter in his own right. The yeti is a formidable opponent; he is strong, stronger than the five craziest men on your expedition. He is loud, louder than a battleship siren when enraged. He can count to ten, but seldom has reason to. He will "play dumb" when need be, but this beast is no idiot. He will bide his time, chewing a wad of his feces, and wait until you fall asleep. Then he'll rip your head off, play football with your skull and defecate in your pith helmet just for laughs.

Brief encounters show that this primate is a toolmaker and possibly even a user of crude language, as noted by the many epithets in the yeti proto-language. He clearly understands the use of fire, the assemblage of stone weapons, the making of primitive huts, and the rudiments of a simple, barter economy. In this sad world, social status is obtained by an excess of flatulence and the stomping of flowers and any other objects of beauty.

Though our best Anglican missionaries have attempted to raise these white devils out of the gutter, they continue to persist in their barbaric, heathen ways.

The yeti, so it would seem, even practice a primitive form of heathen religion, crafting effigies representing some sort of snow god, upon which are placed macabre idols made of stone, bone and—since the advent of contact with Westerners—toilet paper rolls.

Sesquipedalian language will not be your ally in your encounters with the yeti, but rather a large stick, soft foot-steps and an impatient father's discipline are the best tools with which to handle these white devils.

Heed the following instructions well, and stray from it not one centimeter.

Brook no trade. Other, unscrupulous explorers have plied the wily yeti with boxes of cigarettes and stacks of por-nography in exchange for yeti mountain gold. A gentleman never stoops to such despicable tactics.

Always enter a yeti village or cave with your left foot forward. In yeti culture, the right foot is extremely flexible and always used for self-abuse and thus, entering a room with the right foot forward is a token of extreme disrespect.

Before entering any village, set up a maxing gun, a Browning or other mechanized weapon in a camouflaged location on the perimeter. If for some odd reason the yeti refuse to divulge the location of their gold stores, or refuse to accept Christ as their savior, it is ethically permissible to annihilate the village.

Diplomacy should always proceed from the opened bible or the barrel of a loaded .303.

Upon training riles on the village, the expedition leader should open his yeti-phrasebook bible and read in a clear, audible voice. In exchange for all of their gold, and the immediate shedding of their heathen and barbarian ways, the yeti should be promised eternal salvation in the next life (you need not believe it) and free haircuts, as well as education, fair governance, clean drinking water, a flat tax, electric lights, and paved streets.

If the yeti fail to respond to your reasonable requests and generous offer, then explode multi-colored fireworks over their heads, and explain to them that their gods are offended by their impudence.

On occasion, the yeti may be placated by the use of a female yeti decoy, sprayed with copious amounts of musky female yeti estrous scent. As the males attempt to complete for the privilege of mating with the decoy, the expedition leader can deploy a man deep into the yeti cave to dig for gold.

Should it become necessary to terminate an entire yeti village, use the phrase "unfortunate incident" when describing the event to the press or to the Home Office.

When given half a chance, the yeti will not hesitate to eat you, so therefore consider yourself at liberty to eat the yeti when deemed expedient or appropriate.

Remember, the yeti have no concept of personal property

and his childlike intelligence is incapable of discerning the value or use of gold. Therefore, gentlemen mountaineers do him a great service in relieving him of his burden. In order to satisfy the yeti's insatiable demand for shiny objects, offer him baubles such as carnival park souvenir shot glasses, plastic mood rings, and gold-colored painted, cast iron necklaces encrusted with glass diamonds.

If junk and baubles cannot hold his fickle attention, offer the yeti one hour of "puppy time" with a basketful of puppies for every troy ounce of gold nougat removed from the treasure caves. If the yeti should attempt to rough-handle or eat any of the puppies, don't hesitate to exterminate them with the maxing gun.

Here are some convenient yeti phrases:

WAH! RAAAAAR! ARRRRR-ARRRR-ARRR! UP-AHHHHHHHH! PLOP! JESIM CRACK!
We come bearing the good tidings of Jesus the Christ.

SNICK! SNIT, SPIT, SNAAAAAAAAA-UH-AH-UH-AH-UH-AH!
Repent your heathen ways and forsake your idols or you will feel the wrath of our mighty thunder bucket.

RAAR, NAH, BAH! BLAH, BLAH, BLAH! HUUUP! OOOOOOOH AHHHHHH!
We have brought you this fine woman. Her mighty birth

canal could squeeze out a yak. Look, her hips are wider than the mighty Blah! River that crosses your territory! Her breasts are so large they could suffocate a herd of rams. She will surely take your bifurcated member with extreme pleasure. Give us all your gold and she is yours.

INT-AH-LA! YUR, NERT BLURT, BLAH. HUP, JURP. QUIRP, QUIRP. OOOH, RA! THUP NUP.

If you accept us as your sovereign masters, we will show mercy, and fit your cave with electric lights and wireless internet.

URP URP! GRONK BONK BURP SMURP. EEEEEEEEE-UH! GREEP NEEP HUP! AB-RAM!

You have offended the Great White Father, and now he responds with many arrows of death. His thunder bucket quivers with disconsolate rage. Prepare to meet the god of Abraham.

THEEN MOP CMOP BEBOP. MOHO, PEO OOMBOP? KAWA-NINT, COPM? EROP HRAM GNOP?

Please tell us what your values and roles are. How do you bide your leisure time? What activities of daily living give you satisfaction? What are your short-term goals for our encounter?

RIMRAM, JUNOOT. DEET LOP TOP. CREEP CRAM DAM GROP NOP!

We promise a university education to every first-born son.

Oo-lop! Rim pop, bee-bop, mop, mop! Creea Vromp, klomp!

You must stop eating dung, including your own. This is more filthy than self-abuse. If you must eat dung, than use these breath mints or we can no longer parlay with you.

Gwar-mon, Hron, mimp, yon yop. Frump dump, Gwar-mon!

No, you are not a Mormon. You may not take many wives. The Mormons no longer do that.

Nee-up nuh pooh-pee towm yup nar vrop. Int lop pooh-pee towm-ah.

You will be given one hour of puppy time for every troy ounce of gold we remove for your treasure cave. You must never eat the puppies during puppy time.

Eeep peep? Eeep peep? Ha! Yun eeep!

Fuck me? Fuck me? No, fuck you.

PENGUINS MAKE CAPITAL PACK ANIMALS

Selecting appropriate expedition animals, as well as the right people to handle them is a matter of great import, for animals can mean fresh meat, produce, entertainment, and companionship, and their lack can mean the difference between a banquet versus begging alms.

The first thing to note, is climate. No expedition should proceed with animals unfit for the adventuring climate. Since however, mountain goats, bears, and picas can be notoriously difficult to corral, one must choose animals who are veterans of the cold, polar regions, critters with heavy coats and stout bodies, easily tamed, and no threat to man.

While as yet untried, it seems logical to assume that penguins are the best choice for the rigors of mountaineering. Their climbing abilities have not been tested, but their natural docility, calm demeanor and ability to obey simple commands make them a wise choice. Also, their silly, clownish antics are a delight for all to see. While the pack burdens they carry are less than an infant human, if enough penguins are deployed, virtually every piece of gear may safely ascend to the heights fully intact.

For those objects deemed too large to fit in a single penguin pack, you may harness two, five, or ten, fifty or more penguins together in order to shoulder the burden. In order to determine the total number of penguins needed for an expedition, take the total number of men and multiple it by the number of days the expedition is expected to last, then add 178. Then subtract 1 penguin for every day at 65 degrees F or above. Aha! You have arrived at the correct number of penguins!

Of course, you do realize that penguins have culinary and spiritual needs that must be attended to.

Each penguin requires one salted kipper per meal and at bedtime, one half kipper for penguins who have been good. Being "good" means that each penguin is expected to haul cargo up the mountain for 15 hours per day in their backpacks. Additionally, they must be ready to be eaten at the behest of the explorers: penguin fatty cakes with flipper sandwiches are a prized delicacy, and spotted dick fried in penguin blubber is most delectable.

Penguins—ironically—are terribly scattered, flighty

little things, who become confused easily. Therefore, penguin discipline is an utmost priority. Each morning, every penguin regiment must rise for the raising of the Union Jack, and chirp their best rendition of God Save the Queen as best they can. Then, they must do 40 jumping jacks, 15 burpees, and 25 rounds with the hoola hoop. After breakfast, they will practice marching, parade drilling, and band practice with fife and drum. Awards will be given to the best drummers, and push-ups and yelling will be the reward for slow and clumsy penguins.

At the beginning of each meal and before bed time, penguins will select one of their brethren to the role of Expedition Vicar Penguin, who will lead them all in grace, and take their confession. All penguins will kneel, fold their flippers, and praise Jesus as best their limited squeaks and grunts will allow. All those who shirk prayers or are seen worshipping the penguin fish god will be beaten and eaten.

By the conclusion of the expedition, most penguins will have been eaten anyway.

Before eating your penguins, be sure that you have at least a few lactating females around, for nothing is sweeter than tea flavored with penguin milk. Though a bit on the fishy side, penguin milk is rich in fats and a great source of calcium. Of course, milking a penguin can be a bit difficult. In order to do so, the adventurer must locate the row of small, marble-sized teats protruding from the teat sack on the abdomen of the pregnant female. Then, whilst holding a pail or jug, the explorer should give a firm tug on each of the six teats, one after the other. Each penguin should yield about one pint of penguin milk per day, quite enough to supply the gentlemen, the puppies, and the kitty cats of the perilous expedition into the unknown.

All penguins should be trained to tuck explorers into bed at night, and to clean up after the puppies. They should be able to beguile with their silly antics, balance red rubber balls on their beaks, but also able to shoulder a pack at a moment's notice, and take up arms against the yeti.

Speaking of puppies, each expedition should be provisioned with one basketful of adorable puppies per explorer. Puppies facilitate comfort, warmth, and can be worn alive by being placed into a "puppy coat." The expedition puppy master should be a stern yet stout-hearted soul, one who is used to adversity in all things related to puppy care. Unlike the penguins, the puppies are excused from puppy prayers because puppies are natural heathens. However, the expedition puppies must be able to provide warmth,

comfort, and "puppy sniffles" to the explorer everyday, or else they must be shamed. As previously noted, puppies are also useful as a bargaining tool with the yeti. The yeti can be promised one hour of "puppy time" for every troy ounce of mountain gold offered up to the explorer party.

The penguins should be fitted with wicker baskets with back pack straps in order to secure the puppies for each leg of the ascent.

Another animal that must make its way to the heights is the horse, for nothing is so noble as "stallion steak." The horse may be viewed as a walking, neighing meat stick with legs and hooves. Every effort should be made to secure horse meat for the penguins, the men, and the puppies, as well as the kitty cats, who often say, "meow likes a big, fat horsey steak." The expedition horses should never bear burdens of any weight, lest it render their delicate meat tough and impliable.

Speaking of pussy cats, no expedition is complete without five or six naughty cats who frolic about in the snow, and steal the occasional can of kippers. The kitty cats should be trained to wear woolen knickers and leather boots. With enough training, even the most sullen pussy can be trained to meow in time to God Save the Queen during the raising of the colors, with cap off, of course. Unlike the penguins, which are often content to frolic in their own wretched filth, Sir Robert Baden Powell once said, "there is no such thing as a dirty pussy! Indeed the only thing I have seen a pussy discharge is his Enfield carbine!"

Along with the cats, a supply of rats and rabbits should be brought up the mountain, for nothing so occupies a mischievous pussy than chasing a rat around a glacier. As for the bunny rabbits, they, like the puppies, provide a comfort to the explorer. What rugged, careworn chap wouldn't like to see a docile bunny face peeking through his tent flaps each morning while he takes his morning glass of penguin milk.

Along with the puppy master and the penguin tamer, a rat releaser, horse cook, and bunny buster should also accompany the expedition in the field.

A good field commander understands the value of a solid English breakfast! Without breakfast, no one can do anything useful. Therefore, skip breakfast at your peril. A good breakfast consists always of the following:

Main Course

Fatty cakes sandwich, with fried flipper "bread"
Fricasseed horse flank steak

Second Course

2 penguin eggs, par boiled
1 tin, spotted dick fried in penguin fat
1 cup of strong tea

Dessert

1 spoonful of "expedition snuff"
(powdered, mild tobacco leaf mixed with cocaine)
1 pipeful of mild tobacco
1 cup penguin milk, collected fresh daily

ON THE MERITS OF CANNIBALISM

The Custom of the Sea provides for a solution to unfortunate situations in which shipwreck survivors cast lots in order to determine who will provision a food source for the remaining group members. Cannibalism is often viewed as a difficult, shameful experience to both the cannibalizer and the cannibalisee, yet it need not always be so.

The Custom of the Mountain is a code similar to the Custom of the Sea, but while cannibalism may be Custom of the Sea, orderly cannibalism based on rank and title is the more gentlemanly, civilized Custom of the Mountain.

It must be stated as a forethought, that this peculiar ritual should never be invoked but out of the direst necessity. Only after the horse meat is gone, the penguins, rats and rabbits are depleted, should it be invoked. Whatever happens, never eat the puppies. A gentleman never eats puppies out of his love for the innocent.

When all his resources are gone, after every horse, penguin, rat, mountain goat, cat, and yeti has been eaten, a gentleman has no recourse but to consume his men. He should take care to only eat the lowliest first, the criminals, the insane and the servants. Start with the tanners, water bearers, and dung stove tenders, and work your way up to the officers. However, save the cook for last, especially if he is particularly keen at his trade. He should be last, going even before the other officers going first.

Explorers have two options for initiating The Custom of the Mountain. First, wait until the first man of lesser rank expires, and eat him, OR wait until the first hunger pangs appear, and order the lower ranked men to draw straws. Please refer to the pyramid below in order to understand the order of those to be eaten.

If, after the first hunger pangs, no one dies, the edible men are to draw straws from the expedition straw drawing kit. The man who draws the shortest straw forfeits his life, while the man who draws the second shortest straw agrees to shoot the first man. All other men agree to eat the shortest straw drawer, but ONLY after he is dead.

The commander should specify that under no circumstances are the brain or gonads of the dead men to be eaten, as this is sacrilege. Instead, these should be given a Christian burial along with the clothing and personal effects of the deceased. Before dispatching the unlucky recipient of the short straw, hand him a copy of Dr. Browntrout's Unabridged Guide to Suggested Last Words and Final Statements for the Doomed, the Damned and the Dying. Open the book and turn to the chapter on Custom of the Mountain. Also, ascertain what manner of death he would prefer his wife and children to believe felled him. Suggest a steep fall while summiting, or death in battle against the yeti, or some other appropriately manly end.

If it should come to pass that all in the expedition have been eaten but the officers, then they too must draw straws and hold themselves subject to The Custom of the Mountain. After the commander and his first officer are the only surviving members of the expedition, the commander can elect to shoot and eat the first officer, or both can shake hands and agree to shoot each other at the same time and be done with the whole horrid business.

Once the commander is the sole surviving member of the expedition, all is not lost, for there are still options! The commander may elect to end his suffering at once, or, if he possesses the steely resolve to go on, he can elect to take one teaspoon of Mrs. Right–A–Way's Tincture of Opium Cure All. He may then use the expedition amputation saw (or his katana) and take off one of his limbs, and eat that. If, after eating a leg, help or rescue has not arrived, the commander certainly has nothing to lose by taking off another leg. Here, it must be stated that it would be wise to not be too picky about gristle or fat. Indeed, "waste not, want not" must be our motto in this situation, as well as, "god helps those who help their selves."

If, indeed, no help at all is forthcoming after the second leg, then by all means, take off an arm, taking care to take off the non-dominant arm with the dominant arm. If this comes to pass, and several more days yet go by when no help or rescue seems forthcoming, the expedition commander may wish to reevaluate the situation.

He may wish to use his remaining limb to write a letter to his wife, explaining that a somewhat unfortunate incident befall him and his expedition, and that some minor difficulties happened to make a bit of a bump in the road. He should state that nothing bad has happened at all, but rather a slight delay may prevent the two of them meeting on this side of St. Peter's Gate.

Then, the expedition commander should feel at liberty to gnaw upon his remaining limb until he finds it no longer serviceable.

THE EXPEDITION FOOD HIERARCHY, A.K.A.. WHO EATS WHO? WHO EATS YOU?

Remember, puppies should NEVER be eaten, but if they are starving, they should be dispatched with a pistol and laid to rest in a cold, puppy grave.

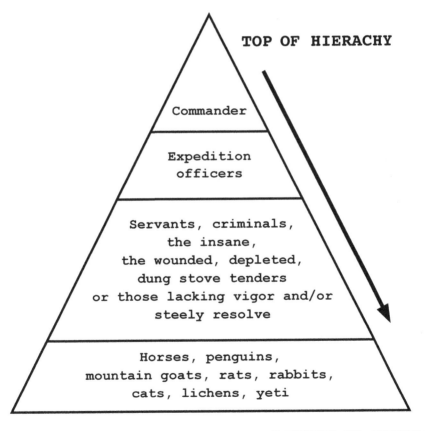

TOP OF HIERACHY

Commander

Expedition officers

Servants, criminals, the insane, the wounded, depleted, dung stove tenders or those lacking vigor and/or steely resolve

Horses, penguins, mountain goats, rats, rabbits, cats, lichens, yeti

BOTTOM OF HIERACHY

CREVASSIGATION: Finding Your Way About On The Mountain

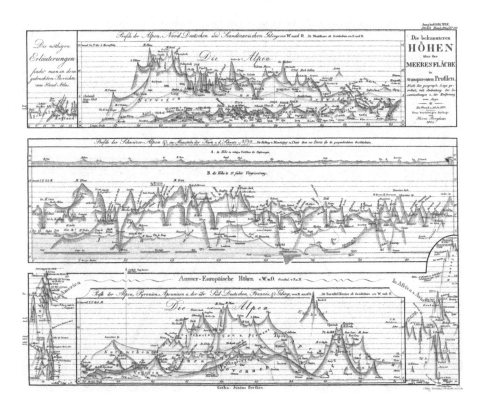

These are the nuts and bolts of mountaineering. Forget about the bolts for a minute, because you're going to have to have nuts and be nuts in order to keep from bolting. Is any of this getting through to you? Okay, good. First thing: here's how you find your way on a mountain.

If you are at the bottom of a mountain, go up it.

If you are on top of a mountain, go down it.

Never retreat from a retreating glacier because
that is when the glacier is weakest.

Never pussyfoot around a crevasse:
jump straight over it at the widest point
while waving around your katana.
If the crevasse is too wide to jump, then go down
to the bottom and up the other side.
Real men don't shy away from these blue holes
of death, they conquer them!

If a rock fall seems likely, stand in
the fighting stance, ready with your katana.
Swipe at any boulder headed your way.
Let the mountain know that it is
your time to kick ass and take names.

Knock down any seracs (ice towers) you see
using dynamite or plastic explosives.

Although the sun usually sets in the west,
on mountains it rises in the east.

Lumps of fox scat always face south in spring,
north in winter.

In a whiteout, ignite multi-colored smoke grenades
in order to provide visual contrast.

In order to navigate properly, leave your map and compass at home. You must learn to see the mountain, memorize the terrain, and create a mental image which will then become a mental map. Maps are two-dimensional depictions of our planet, earth. Two-dimensional thinking involves seeing the earth as latitudinal and longitudinal intersections of lines that form chains of intersecting squares, which then become one large grid. Mountains, however are three-dimensional forms that require you to mentally metamorphose the squares you just imagined into boxes, or cubes. For every direction in which you turn your gaze, visualize a series of uniformly shaped, stacked cubes covering all that your vision encompasses. Now take a finger and hold it up at the midline of your face, at arms' length. Your finger is now "point zero," the center of the planet, nay the center of the known universe. Now, take the same finger from the other hand and place it atop the first finger, forming a "T". Close one eye and squint across your "T". The point at which the two fingers cross is the corner of the known universe.

Move the "T" slowly and you turn 360 degrees, mentally mapping everything you see. Take "mental pictures" quickly of each mountain feature, assigning numerical values to every point and line of your cubes. It may help to know that every mountain has ruffles and wrinkles. Each of the ruffles is a canyon, gulch or a fan. Each wrinkle is the fold of a lateral moraine, a couloir or cirque. Visualize yourself carefully unfolding each of these wrinkles and ruffles, and suddenly your complex, three-dimensional map of cubes has once more become a manageable, simple two-dimensional plane.

Now, there is one last feature that must be added to the map: YOU. You are the fourth dimension. Envision a red dot moving rapidly through every cube, ruffle, wrinkle, line and square. Imagine the red dot moving, like the laser sight of a high-powered rifle, coldly and determinedly toward the summit of the mountain until it has been attained. Now, you will never more fear of losing your way.

HOW TO PROPERLY RECORD YOUR MANLY ADVENTURE IN A LEATHER BOUND JOURNAL

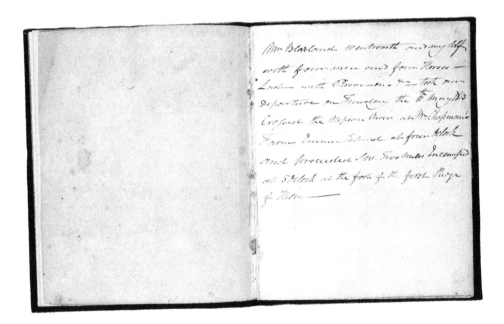

Should you die up there, this is the most important chapter of the book—mine and yours! As previously noted, a journal is not a diary. The only feelings mentioned in a journal are steely resolve, stoic determination to weather all adversity, and brief goodbyes to family members (keep it brief). This is your acid-resistant means of documenting your progress, and for stating what it was that killed you. Be sure to note the time and date of the moment you took the summit, so that it can be etched on to your tombstone, for future generations of real men to see. Study the manliness style guide below for do's and don'ts regarding the art of adventure journaling. A typical entry is short, succinct, almost terse. Let the reader beg for more; don't just give it to him all at once.

Example #1: Opening An Entry

Correct:

The date is 2/17/2056. Time: 3:07 p.m. Ascended Dead Man's Plateau at an even pace, now moving forward to No Return Ridge. Coughed once after ascending to 12,000 feet from sea level, but otherwise all body systems intact. Sharpened my carbonized, steel axe head in preparation for the final push tomorrow at dawn. Now to go to bed standing bolt-upright.

Incorrect:

Dear Diary, I'm so sad when I'm away from my girlfriend. Sometimes I wonder if I should really be here. Man, who am I next to a big, scary mountain? Nobody, that's who. The other guys laughed at me when I pooped into the blue bag that I have to take down the mountain. You know, that really hurt my feelings! I just want to get along here man. I just want to, you know, feel some sort of presence?

Notice how the second entry said almost nothing but it contains twice as many words as the first entry? The first entry gave every relevant, concrete detail, and even managed to bestow a little glimmer of honor and Glory on the writer, even though he had not even summited yet. Can you say that about the writer of the second entry? Definitely not. Is this man a total pussy, or has he simply not mastered the art of adventure journaling? We'll never know, because he's probably dead in a hole somewhere.

Example #2: How To Describe Forbidding Terrain

Correct:

Team Alpha One Kick-Ass traversed another behemoth glacier while boulders careened from thousands of feet above us. One of the team bought it right there. Poor bastard caught a curveball from the hand of Satan. The rock split his helmet and cracked his skull like an eggshell. The team tried to stuff his brain back into his head, but it just oozed out like a giant, brown booger. We covered him in snow and put a tag on his toe in case the vultures tried to eat his face off. The team assembled and mooned his corpse in tribute before moving on. If Donny's spirit was watching, it smiled and gave us the finger.

Incorrect:

The team walked across the glacier. The glacier was big. The glacier had ice. The ice was big. So was the glacier. A rock fell and a valued team membered passed away after we tried some first-aid. We cried for hours and hours. It was just so sad. There was a lot of crying. And hugging, so much hugging. Gentle Bill McWilly pulled out his guitar and sang some really moving folk songs while our tears froze to our eyelashes. A few of us flicked our lighters.

Did you notice anything about the second entry? How

the team crosses forbidding terrain is the story of the adventure. This is the time to grease up the story with powerful metaphors and similes to highlight the action in the narrative. What kind of pissant says that they "walked" across a glacier? No real man ever "walks" anywhere! You traverse, bound, bolt, shimmy, blaze, blast, hell even stagger, but walk? No my friend, walking is for pussies! Notice also how in the second entry they referred to their friend as "passing away." Ridiculous! No one passes away on a mountain. They die horribly. Your readers will fall asleep like a kitten by a fireplace who just had a glass of warm milk unless you talk about death using vivid depictions of the Three B's: blood, brains, bones.

Example #3: Describing Your Last Moments/Leaving Your Legacy In Words

This is the most important function of your leather-bound, acid-resistant adventure journal, and it bears careful consideration. Your final journal entry is the lasting impression you will give to the entire world, to say nothing of your family and your man friends. Choose your words wisely. Better to die silently and leave no trace than to die sounding like a whiney-ass little bitch for all eternity.

Correct:
The entrance to the ice-cave fell in about an hour ago. My legs are slightly impaired from being snapped in multiple places by a frisky yeti, but do not fear for I feel nothing but gratitude for having made it thus far. The yeti that has temporarily detained

me has no powers of speech, but he keeps fondling my balls, then pointing to a cauldron of boiling liquid, then patting his belly and grunting. I'm sure it is just a silly game from a playful mountain primate, and nothing that should concern anyone at home. I just want Dolly and Martha to understand that it may be a little while before daddy can pick out those ponies for their birthdays. Tell Dolly that daddy thinks Butterscotch is a fine name for a pony, a real dandy of a name. Tell her to take real good care of Butterscotch, and to empty out his litterbox every-day, because until daddy can come home Butterscotch will be a pony angel who takes good care of those girls. And Cindy, one more thing: you were a good wife, you always cleaned up after me, but this is one mess I made that only God and Jesus can clean up. With dearest, kindest loving sentiments, I remain your be-loved paw-paw and hubby. — P

Incorrect:

I'm so tired and weak. My delicate, sensitive man-hands are trembling from the exquisite pain which has no end. I busted my coccyx on that last fall, and if that wasn't enough, my hemor-rhoid is as big as a smurf-tail. I smoked a ton of weed, but my shit stills seems so fucked up. Why did I have to climb that ridge? Why did I even come to this stupid mountain? Jimmy, if you're reading this, please throw away my anal beads, my plastic va-gina and the German S & M mags before mom goes through my shit. (Actually, keep the beads if you want; they're loads of fun, but be careful because the third one's coming loose.) That's not how I want to be remembered. There's some really gross stuff in there, but I was bored you know? By the way, you can tell Henry that I was the one who took a leak in his graphics bong, and it's *still funny that motherfucker smoked a quarter through my piss bubbles before he realized what was up. Oh shit! Man, this shit is like, so unfair! I shouldn't have to die, not when I'm so young.*

As you can glean from these heady examples of death narratives, whining, begging and confessing are the worst and least honorable means by which to discuss the immanent snuffing out of your man-flame. The death-narrative is not the time to cry, to gloat, to blame others, to admit to any but the most mild and perfunctory experiences of physical or mental discomfort. It IS however, the time to bid fond farewell to your wife and children, and to get religion.

Action Verbs For Mountain Writing:

The Climb:

Weak: walked, shuffled, moved

Strong: traversed, ambled, scrambled, bounced, blasted, shimmied, staggered, blazed

The Summit:

Weak: summited, approached, reached, attained, obtained

Strong: took, defiled, destroyed, conquered, owned, stole, smote, slew, dominated, killed, annihilated, smashed, bombed

Death:

Weak: passed on, passed away, moved on to a better place, left his/her earthy body, expired, no longer with us anymore

Strong: bit it, bought it, snuffed, smooshed, crushed, crunched, terminated, wiped out, plummeted, broke into pieces, ripped apart, exploded, mangled, got sucked into the void, caught some air, cratered, eviscerated, mangled

Weather Conditions:

Weak: blew, snowed, hailed

Strong: scoured, whipped, blasted, tormented, howled, shot

Miscellaneous expletives:

Weak: could be better, darned, oofda, oh geez, joshed, stuffed

Strong: terminally fucked, asshole down a crevasse hole, kittywampus, ass over ankles, noggin knocker, fracked up, bouillabaised, dilly barred, shot down on dookie creek, dank-free and cranky, gone tits up (UK), goofy tunes, pulled a hickory dick, pasted out in the jam, pulled a floppy eagle, free booted, kissed the crater, gone back to the six mile seven.

ESTABLISHING DOMINION OVER NATURE

In the bible it says, "smite every living thing that creepeth." To that, this author adds an emphatic "damn right!" By "creepeth," we also mean things that run, skitter, fly, crawl or gambol about. Birds and mammals are unnatural when they approach mountains, and their presence is often damaging to the fragile glacier. Give Mother Nature a helping hand once in awhile by helping to dispatch creatures that have a hatred of man with the use of the .44, the blowgun, the axe or by trap, snare, seine or net.

The wildness of creatures is what makes them unpredictable, foolish, and prone to attack. Do not wait for a warning sign. A gentleman always forms ranks and brandishes his weapon, challenging offensive creatures to a civilized duel. If the creature fails to respond, you are honor-bound to fire at-will until your ammunition is expended or the creature is killed.

Be especially wary of the wily yeti, or snow-daemon. He may attempt to arouse your sympathies, but he is rouge and a scamp, and he will attempt to bedevil you with primate trickery. Do not share your food with him, or sell him any trinkets from your mess kit. These beasts are known far and wide for spending climbers' coin on cigarettes and pornography. The moment you encounter a yeti or its brood, promptly hack them to death using your katana, battle-axe or spiked-mace.

SEIZING UNSPOILED BOUNTY FROM THE BOSOM OF THE MOUNTAIN

Mountaineering is an expensive endeavor. Being a gentleman is an expensive endeavor. An authentic katana alone can cost thousands of dollars, and you won't find a .44 pistol at the local dimestore. Those of us who wish to tame the heights must hope that we are highborn to Old Money. But what of the rest of us, born of the slums, denizens of the middle-class ghetto? Do we who do not have our slippery fingers on the fickle teats of the Money Cow have any chance to avoid the horrors of a debtors' prison upon our return from the summit?

The answer is yes! In the days of yore, prospectors showed up to gold-soaked rivers barefoot in feces-besmirched potato sacks, and left their claims wearing seersucker suits and wingtips. The trick is to let the mountain pay your way. Any geologist will tell you that mountains are full of minerals—not just gold. By carrying plastic explosives, one can start a strip-mining operation on almost any mountain. Simply dig a cat-hole using your trenching spade, pop in the explosives and let 'er rip! The discovery of gold, silver, copper or bronze can easily pay off the balance due on your premium camping outlet store credit card, or the loan for your expedition transport vehicle.

A mountain is full of minerals, but your supply of explosives is limited. The question is, therefore, how does one find the most valuable minerals on the mountain with the least effort? The answer is simple: by use of a dowsing stick! In the old days, treasure hunters used dowsing sticks and seer stones to ascertain the whereabouts of water and buried treasure.

Indeed, these methods are still used today throughout the world, and educated people need not shy away from these scientifically sound methods just because they resemble superstitions of yore. In the olden times, people prayed and chanted over their sticks and stones in the hope of enlisting the aid of divine providence for use in assisting with their earthly endeavors, but today the practice is much simpler and more correct.

The modern method is as follows: Find a forked stick and two smooth stones. Set the stick on its end. Ask the stick, "can you find what I seek?" and see if the stick reacts in any way. If the stick moves even slightly, this is the affirmative response. Repeat the same steps for potential seer stones. Once you have determined by this method that your stick and/or stones are suitable treasure locating devices, hold them in your hand and command them thusly:

Seer stone or seer stick
Find my way through murky thick
Part the trees to take a peek
At buried booty that I seek
Scatter rocks and earth and dust.
From down below, up treasure thrust.

The use of this command has been proven in randomized controlled trials to produce satisfactory results at least 50% of the time.

STEPPING OVER THE CORPSES OF THE WEAK, THE MEEK AND THE MILD

When you reach certain, forbidding areas, you will see the bones of those who came to conquer before you. They're all dead now. Their mummified remains are scattered about in the Death Zone, where all life is bound to fail, where the air itself will not sustain the strongest among us.

You must prepare to add your corpse to the corpse pile.

But before you do that, step over the dead ones and continue on, knowing that you went further and lasted longer than your deceased brethren conquerors. The mountain gods have smote them and they have their eye on you too. The vultures hover ever closer, waiting their turn to pry your tight flesh out of the trendy neon orange goose down jacket that flaps around your lifeless body in the cruel wind. Your day will come. But until then, until the evil gods make cruel sport of your ragged skeleton, stand up and shake your fist at them. Step over the corpses of the weak, the meek and the mild, not somberly, but with self-adoration and confidence!

BOOTSTRAPS, AND WHAT THEY'RE FOR

What are bootstraps? You know damn well what they are. They're straps of leather on the sides of your boots for pulling yourself up and erect. When you get your panties in a bind, when you feel like a cup of warm milk, when you need to man-up in a hurry, just remember: that's what bootstraps are for.

NO, IT'S NOT OKAY TO CRY

There are times when it hurts so damned bad that your lower man-lip might begin to tremble. You must check that! If you let that lip tremble too much, an ugly, vile man-tear might roll down your man-face. And then what would happen? Soon, you'll be blubbering all day and night until you roll off the mountain and over to some sort of support group for broken pansies with no self-control. Crying causes severe dehydration. Being a man means always being in control. If you feel like crying: just don't.

Crying is what women do, and they aren't men. It is more manly to poop your pants than to cry, so do that instead. Crying lets the mountain know that you're a soft-bellied loser. Is that what you want? If you feel like crying, pinch your nut-sack really hard. Then you'll have something to cry about.

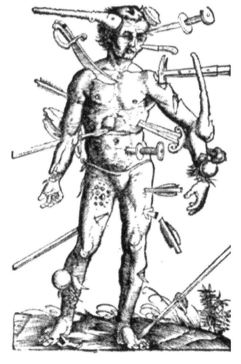

WHEN DEATH IS IMMINENT, FIGHT DEATH TO THE DEATH!

There will be times and places where death seems to have you in its icy, death-like grasp. You will be falling, ass-over-tea kettle into a bottomless crevasse, or your rope suddenly breaks, dropping you into spinning freefall into a gaping chasm of doom, or perhaps a starving yeti suddenly appears from behind, wielding a boulder and gnashing its grimy teeth. Are these the times to let go, to beg your guardian penguin for help, to call your wife to say good-bye? How would that sound, anyway?

"Hi honey, I'm going to have to make this a quick one.

See, I only have about five more seconds left before—."

Or

"Honey, remember those pictures of huge footprints I uploaded to the facebook, well, uh, it seems—COINK!"

No, no and no!

When death rears its ugly head, fight it on your own terms, in the time and place of your own choosing. Death will not wait for your answer—unless you give Death your answer in a firm, stern tone of voice. Once you have had time to gather your wits, pull out all of your weapons. Dig your heels in. Swing wildly, and if that fails: swing again. If you find yourself falling—screw self-arrest—use your indomitable will to create the friction required to slow you down.

If a yeti attacks from behind, make eye contact with the rogue, and use the power of animal magnetism to sedate it, then take off its head with one, deft swipe from the katana. Then find the beasts' nest and slay its entire brood. If hypoxia sets in, breathe harder, until your lungs fill with enough air. If hypothermia sets in, use your will and steely resolve to light a fire on the mountain. This is the way real men cheat death and steal Glory.

WHEN DEATH IS CERTAIN, DON'T TAKE IT LYING DOWN

There is but one time when there is no escape from death, and that is when death is certain. Before determining this to be the case, take stock of the situation. Be sure you are about to die before you are about to die. Is the avalanche that buried you really that deep? Are you suffocating under the snow, or just panicking? Are all of your arms and legs broken after plunging into the crevasse, or are you simply having a bout of unmanliness preventing your hard climb out of the jaws of the abyss?

If death really IS certain, know this: you still have options. You can prepare. You can choose how you wish to be remembered. For one thing, don't lie down! Stand up and die like a man! Die reaching for Glory! But before you do that, take a few notes and write some stoic goodbyes in your leather bound, acid-resistant journal (not diary), seal it in a deerskin chamois, and tuck it in the middle layer of your clothing (so that your rotting corpse does not degrade the paper). If at all possible, prepare and drink as much tea as you can, and then eat the tea bags. This will fill you with enough tannins to preserve your body as a final memorial to your honor and glory.

Only after these steps have been completed can you relax and take your final breaths. If you have a locket with a photograph of a loved one, feel free to open it and gaze upon it as the last spark of your life force exits your earthly body.

SMITING THE SUMMIT!

On occasion, one finds oneself in a situation in which death is not certain or imminent, a situation in which there are no grave injuries, no bouts of mountain insanity—a situation where the summit tarries no longer in the distant horizon, but just a few feet from your face. On such rare occasions, Glory is yours for the taking without the onerous snake of death nipping at your toenails. A gentleman mountaineer must be equally prepared to seize Glory as he is ready to accept Death.

The summit is the place where Glory lives and breathes! It is the place where the mountain can no longer touch you, where you can gaze down its—once forbidding, now lowly—flanks with mocking, antidisestablishmentarian contempt and make cruel sport of that object and those gods which would have made cruel sport of you. Upon conquering a summit, no longer is death a possibility.

From here, you may relax in the idyllic mountain air and contemplate a laconic descent after gamboling about like a charging stallion on the newly-tamed peak. Indeed, once a summit is bagged, the end of the rainbow is reached and like a mischievous leprechaun stealing a pot of gold, you too may dance a conquering jig whilst imitating the sound of flatulence.

Though by no means is it to be expected or guaranteed, a gentleman must always be prepared for the possibility of stealing Glory from the summit. As with all matters of honor, by no means is simply planting a foot on the summit sufficient to wring Glory from the highest point of the mountain. One may hold an orange in one's hand, but holding the orange is not the same as making orange juice. To make juice, one must beat the orange to a pulp and squeeze the life out of it. As with oranges, so it is with mountains.

In order to squeeze all the Glory out of your mountain summit, you will need to prepare your summit kit in advance, and train for what you need to do in order to use it to maximum effect.

Here are the items you will need in your summit bagging kit:

20 ft. flagpole with flag—this will be used in order to claim ownership over the peak and to assert your authority over the entire massif. Your pole should be completely rigid, erect and made from the hardest materials known to man. Your flag should display your family seal, crest and coat-of-arms in bright colors adorned by flashing, solar-powered signal beacons that will be visible to passing airborne objects at night. It should also have three or four golden tassels, and be topped by a brass stauette of a griffon devouring a yeti.

Rock carving tools—it is absolutely imperative that you carve your name and titles into the stone face nearest the summit with the time, date and length and girth of your penis in metric as well as standard measurements. Choose a granite or marble face if one permits. In fact, if possible, your expedition sculptor should carve an 8-12 meter penile monolith with a bifurcated tip with your name etched at the throbbing base.

Expedition sculptor—this person is a classically trained artist who will render a bust of your head and penis into the surrounding rock using state-of-the-art tools and technology.

Film crew—this is the means by which your Glory will be recorded and transmitted to the unwashed masses seeking inspiration and escape from their hollow lives by being regaled by the stories of the true lives of real men. By no means should the actual summit capture be recorded. No one wants to see tired, sweaty men pant their lungs out while taking baby steps up a mountain. The entire expedition should wash, bathe and apply proper make-up and dress the penguins before the summit scene is recorded, and then climb as quickly and vigorously as possible. Once at the top, the expedition leader should fall to his stomach and begin pelvic-thrusting against the top of the mountain.

Champagne—spirits are absolutely required in order to properly celebrate your victory.

Wreaths of Glory laurels—the mountain can only metaphorically bestow Glory wreaths on you; therefore, come prepared with your own.

CONCLUSION

Now you have all of the tools and social skills you need to succeed in life. Now you know what it means to be a gentleman explorer. You have been trained and educated in the art of wresting Glory from the mountain and if not Glory, then at least an honorable death. The choice between death and glory is not yours to make, but that of the mountain. The choice you have to make is one of honor. Will you comport yourself like a flaccid, sneaky scoundrel or will you beat the mountain into submission, bending millions of tons of rock and ice to conform to the dictates of your will, like a gentleman? Practice your pelvic thrusts. Remember your steely resolve. Swing high your axe. Never shed one tear. Don't ever masturbate. Keep pulling the trigger, and you too may one day find your destiny of death or glory that awaits every man on top of every mountain.

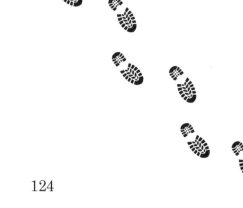

A Kind Word
From Our Sponsor

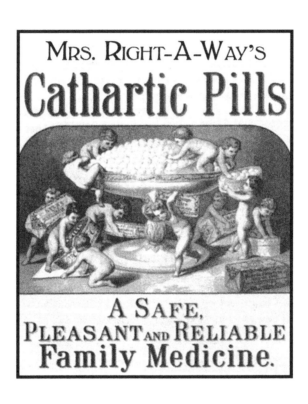

MRS. RIGHT-A-WAY'S
TINCTURE OF OPIUM
Cure All

...A cure for everything that ails everyone!

Mrs. Right-A-Way is the beloved spouse
of a world-renowned physician who has saved
the lives of no fewer than 75,000 INFANTS
and ADULTS suffering from colic, consumption,
monomania, hysteria, piles, hair loss, idiocy,
toothache, headache, trench foot, lunacy, cancer,
diarrhea, dandruff, morbid ruminations, failure to
thrive, erotomania, scrofula, gout, palsy, worry,
acne, immoral tendencies, swollen gonads,
weak character, tender tonsils, gallbladder
congestion, ingrown toenails and alcoholism.

"I give three spoonfuls to my baby every day!"

Mrs. Right-A-Way's is scientifically proven to:

—Re-grow amputated limbs!

—Boost IQ by 50+ points!

—End the filthy urge for self-abuse!

—Restore eyesight to the blind!

—Increase untapped memory power!

—Restore strength, vigor and stamina
 to weak, pasty limbs!!

—Increase obedience to parents in unnatural children!

—Promote church-going and temperance!

—and EVEN MORE!

MRS. RIGHT-A-WAY'S

FIRST KISS
PISS MIST

for the Young Miss

Fathers, have you watched in dismay as your young daughter's fair eyes followed the adductive arc of a young lad's ripped bicep? Have you seen the foam on the mouths of her suitors, like rabid mammals, their throbbing, aching barrel staves barely contained in their waist coats and cumberbuns? Do you not wish you could...

Stop her first kiss before it starts.

Fathers, you know best. You know that all men are savages and beasts, barely checked in their filthy, carnal urges. What defense is there from rogues and rascals?

The Bible is only of limited use in curbing these HELL-SPAWNED DESIRES OF THE QUIVERING FLESH. Woe to these urges! Woe to the blood that quickens! What recourse has a father to protect the FAIR MAIDENS and their MILKY INNOCENCE from aforementioned URGES AND QUICKENINGS?

You just never know where or when…

TEMPTATION WILL REAR ITS UGLY HEAD

Mrs. Right–A–Way, the wife of a famous physician, and the creator of Mrs. Right–A–Way's Tincture of Opium Cure All, has created another panacea. Mrs. Right–A–Way is an old maid who's LOINS ARE LIKE A RUSTY BEAR TRAP, who has not experienced relations in fifty years because she has mastered the SHOVE AWAY. She understands the dangers faced by comely maidens, barely yet to flower in the ripe blossom of womanhood. That is why, for those whose loins are not like a rusty bear trap, who's pale, flaccid, stick arms cannot perform the shove-away, there is another, wholly better defense of maidenhood:

FIRST KISS PISS MIST FOR THE YOUNG MISS

The "piss" used in this mist consists of a highly scientific formula of laudanum, brandywine and fish as well as equine waste products. Waste, you say? Ah, but Mrs. Right–A–Way understands thrift, and she lets nothing go to waste! All a girl need do is mist a little piss mist on their wrist. Or in their room. Or on their pillow. Or in the face of rogues. No more kisses will be attempted, but BOYS OF IMPECCIBLE CHARACTER will NOT BE DETERRED. First Kiss Piss Mist will thwart petting—light and heavy, and is guaranteed to keep RANDY LADS at least 10 centimeters from your person.

Use it liberally:

At the debutante ball

On a fresh bodice

Before retiring to bed

On your maiden fern

With bath water

When darting in and out of the briar patch

Upon nearing a stout oak

Before attending church services

On a tin of Spotted Dick cakes

When reciting evening prayers

When confronted with the urge to "diddle"

To perfume a letter to a would-be lover

Before and after tea time

Anytime you wish, really.

Fathers, listen. First Kiss Piss Mist for the Young Miss has delayed marriage and preserved maidenhood by ten years or more when used every day, and it has even forced some young ladies into the convent! If you truly care about your daughter's chastity and your own sanity, purchase a large bottle of reasonably priced and unreasonably ripe First Kiss Piss Mist, and rest easy forever more!

A First Kiss Piss Mist for the Young Miss
Angel Choir Song

For every Young Miss
Not ready for her first kiss
For every fetching lass
Who's shinny apple is her ass

For every lovely angel
Who's not ready to try anal
For the Gent who is a Brute
And who does not give a hoot

For the mothers and the fathers
Of the girls who test the waters
When lack of perspicacity
Overrules their chastity

In the name of verisimilitude
Down with all the horny dudes!
When fair innocence is risked
(I think now you get the gist)

There is the one, there is the king,
Shining brighter than Queen Mum's Bling
Lust and Desire it will melt
With this aerosol chastity belt

Just dab a droplet on your wrist
Naughty boys now gag and hiss
Soured suitors step aside
Of your cooter, now deprived

Maidens keep their innocence,
From the paws of randy gents
Oh, this elixir's Heaven Scent
Thanks to Mrs. Right-A-Way
An old maid expert in the Shove Away
For building a patented formula
To make young bucks behave more normula

It grows on you like a cyst
It beats all products on the list
It hits you like a fist
It's endorsed by Jesus Christ?
Were it gone it would be missed
It is Young Miss First Kiss Piss Mist!

TUSK MUSK

A Must For Every Man With A Tusk

Excuse me, are you a REAL MAN?

How do you know?

More importantly, how does your LADY know?

She knows by the scent of your TUSK.

But,

What if your TUSK dangles like a deflated party balloon,

swings like a rusty chain, and smells like sour soy milk?

PARTY OVER.

Brother listen, you've got a problem.

You must MUSK your TUSK!

Tusk Musk Gold Label is clinically aged in oaken casks with a side of USDA choice cut beef, and then mixed with the pheromones of a "live" charging bull and the sweat of an aging Eastern European street fighter from an economically depressed, former Soviet bloc nation—as well as a patented mixture of other enhancing chemicals and elixirs. Many of our bull pheromone collecting interns died or were gouged in order to bring you this

ODE TO MALE VITALITY

Liberally applied to every corner of your man shaft, Tusk Musk Gold Label will heighten her desire to smell your tusk for hour upon sweet hour—and nothing more. Your woman will lie enthralled to your rigid, unbendable, briny, bamboo beef baton. She will be so in awe of the shadow cast by your towering, untrainable flesh tree trunk, she will dedicate a temple to it, sacrifice burnt offerings, recruit members of a NEW RANDY RELIGION and never touch it again!

Be careful! 80% female cocaine addicts chose Tusk Musk over cocaine in scientific studies designed by scientists.**

90% of male Tusk Muskers stated that on the third musking, CONDOMS NO LONGER FIT and they had to wear Mu Mu's because their tusk no longer fit inside conventional trousers, a phenomenon so common, it has a name: TUSK BUST***

So brother, what are you waiting for? Isn't it time you bathed your tusk in a mist of musk?

Get your party on and take the
TUSK MUSK PLEDGE:

I _____, a REAL MAN, promise to musk my tusk with Tusk Musk Gold Label until and unless crotch rot prematurely terminates my phallic plans. I swear by Christ that I will faithfully apply Tusk Musk Gold Label all day and night, until my "tusk" smells like barn filled with not-so-fresh hay. Furthermore, I will randomly musk other tusks in public places in order to spread the Gospel According To Tusk Musk until such time as I am beaten unmercifully. I will pray to the Son of Man to extend the girth of my phallus until I am able to throw and catch a football with it.

*Tusk Musk Gold Label assumes no liability for penile prolapse. Death by breast asphyxiation has occurred. Call a doctor if the following symptoms become painful or persist longer than 12 hours: priapism, endless erection, being chased by hundreds of adoring twenty-year-old women with massive fun bags, exploded condoms, blue balls, numb nuts, crotch rot, shaft shakes, flakey foreskin, scrotal edema, or sudden, inexplicable attraction to beef (erotobovinismus). May contain trace amounts of vodka.

**participants were offered cocaine in order to choose Tusk Musk.
***This condition is not identified in the Physician's Desk Reference or the Diagnostic and Statistical Manual of Mental Disorders.

Appendix A:

FIGHTING SONGS TO AROUSE THE SPIRITS OF THE MEN

Real men break into song whenever the occasion presents itself, when attacking the enemy, when conquering the pitiless gods that rule their fate and the mountain, when faced with death. When the ravages of the windswept alpine hell have laid waste to consciousness and conscience: men sing. We sing for religion. We sing for Queen and country. We sing to discover the eunuchs and the unmanly in the party, and then cast them out after excoriating them mercilessly. We sing to placate the savages we encounter and to calm the inner savage that lives deep inside the breast of every manly chest. Here then, is a compendium of the songs you and your squad will use on all occasions. You may use whatever melody or tune seems best to you, or merely to the limits of your vocal range.

ONWARD

Onward, onward, oi, oi, oi!
To burn, to kill and to destroy!
We touch the waste with Christian flame
To cleanse the hordes and the insane!

Onward, onward, oi, oi, oi!
My Maxim gun is not a toy
It will mow you down in haste
Within our wrath it is encased

The bullets fly whilst infidels flee
Like swarms of angry honey bees
For Queen we kill, for Crown destroy
Shouting, shouting: oi, oi, oi!

OLD NELLY  NAG

Old Nelly with breath like a nag
Was my woman when I was a lad
With eyes glazed from laudanum
O the lads she was sodden 'em
For hay penny stuck in her crag

Old Nelly with a mouth like a nag
Her fun bags did stretch and sag
Slapping my face
Whilst flapping through space
But only when she's on the rag

Old Nelly with a head like a nag
For a minute and five
You could say, 'she's all mine'
And slap her ample behind
Whilst she put on a merry chase
And sat on your face
And squeezed out a fart and a shag

My Bess Tess

Bess Tess she is my .303
She always takes good care of me
Martini-Enfield made her
And providence did name her

Bess Tess is my grandma and my carbine
She'll slaughter to protect the lads on the line
Bess Tess is my own best friend
Should she ever jam it will be the end

Bess Tess sends the fiends back to hell
Tearing through the gates of Hades pell mell
When the yeti attacks, Bess Tess got your back
The harry hellions she shall repel!

Bess Tess, Bess Tess I'm in love I do confess
I don't love my Grandma any less
But she won't smite barbarians with tins
of Spotted Dick
Nor drown the devil in the creek

AMOR  FATI!

Amor Fati, oi, oi, oi!
To the death we do deploy
Imperial steel into the belly of
Her Majesty's enemies from below, above
Using the bodies of our spent lads as a ladder
As our blood across the Union Jack spatters
Once more! Rise up! Amor Fati, oi lads, oi!
Imperial steel we shall deploy!

With one thousand to one odds
We thumb our noses at these sods
Who insult Her Majesty's unsullied name
Tell her we did not die in vain!

Loyal, loyal to the last!
Locked and loaded, holding fast
We send defiant greetings with cannonade
Mad Bastards of the Light Brigade!

Amor fati! Amor fati! Oi, oi, oi!
Our own bodies we do deploy
As missiles at the heathens' convoy
We lived as brothers and die as men
Her Majesty's soldiers to the end!

FIGHT SONG OF HER MAJESTY'S
99TH LIGHT EXPEDITIONARY
ANTI-UNICORN BRIGADE, CIRCA 1908

O razored equine bayonette
Perched atop a mane so effete
Doth rent the armor of the heart
Sending so many boys to the death cart

O spiraled horn of death's disguise
You cut down heroes for your prize
Our Maxim guns we trained on you
You rear and charge as bullets flew

O unicorn of death we do despise
The hell-spawned gaze of your red eyes
Yeti mounted, devil sent
You toppled many of our expedition tents

Although you buck, and bray and kick
Our sturdy tins of Spotted Dick
Our camp you think, your rumpus room
As we open fire, and seal your doom

Appendix B:

REAL MAN HALL OF GLORY

These are examples of real men that you can really get behind. These men bent over backwards to follow their dream. They got on top of their demons and thrust their spear in, sweating rivers of rancid, man-sweat all the while.

TEDDY ROOSEVELT

A rough rider who discovered the jungle. He shot two of every living mammal including panda bears and the last known Steller's sea cow.

EARNEST HEMINGWAY

Divorced eighteen times, went fishing for sharks with a tommy gun, drank whiskey by the barrel, invented bootstraps.

CAPTAIN AHAB

Never allowed reality to interfere with his goals.

CHEWBACCA

A wild man who was mechanically inclined and dislocated many shoulders.

Sir Robert Baden Powell

Invented prison camps and the boyscouts.

Ellen Ripley

Killed an alien in her underwear.

Phineas Gage

Lived after an iron, dynamite tamping rod blew his brains out.

Mikhail Kalashnikov

The inventor of the AK-47 assault rifle, the most durable, rugged machine gun ever built.

The Terminator

Methodical, stoic cyborg with ice-chips for blood who never let an armored car or a police station interfere with his mission.

Achilles

The son of a deathless goddess, he slew thousands during the Trojan war.

Boudica

Though not a man, she could have been one.

Appendix C:

GLOSSARY OF IMPORTANT TERMS

Bravery—taking the biggest risks for the least gain.

Cowardice—failing in one's manly duty, cowering before destiny, retreating from danger with or without just cause.

Destiny—the incorporeal quality of time and space which shapes a man into a man, which provides the tools to develop one's honor, to conquer adversity, and to do battle with and overcome weakness with strength.

Dowsing stick—a forked magical stick, scientifically proven to find water and treasure at least 50% of the time.

Glory—the realization of one's destiny, the perfect alloy of honor, strength and resolve, the conquest of nature and the defeat of one's enemies leading to the total domination of nature and humankind.

Katana—the sword of the mighty Samurai warrior—and one of the few worthy tools of the brave mountaineer. Its purpose in mountaineering is three-fold.

1. to wave around when summiting or leaping over a crevasse. 2. to discipline one's companions. 3. to behead yetis, demons or other foul beasts encountered on the flanks of the towering massif.

Manliness—the quality of manhood that makes a man a man, i.e. strength, steely resolve, bravery, imperialism, violence, stoicism, taciturnity.

Resolve, steely—ice chips in the blood, lead in the cranium that causes a man to never waiver from his task and never falter on the path to meet his destiny and be crowned with wreaths of Glory Laurels, defeat his enemies no matter what the odds and to never allow death to get his icy hands round his thick neck.

Seer stone—like a dowsing stick, but in mineral form
Shoe spikes—an unmanly invention that is sometimes used to create friction between a man and the surface of a glacier.

Three B's—blood, brain, belly. You'll need all three if you want to avoid death and obtain Glory.

Yeti—a troublesome primate resembling a man who attempts to trick climbers and spend the mountaineer's hard-earned coin on cigarettes and pornography.

About Dr. Browntrout

Dr. Browntrout was born in 1837 in the Dakota Territories. He believes in firm but kind correction, and the consistent application of Right Thinking. He cured several outbreaks of idleness on the frontier before being called upon to treat self-abuse induced idiocy on many battlefields of that Great Conflagration known as the Civil War. During the 20th Century he turned his attention to moral improvement through mental effort. Contact him at: HoraceSBrowntrout@gmail.com

"The private parts of all men are dirty, and spread illness through the nefarious spewing of tiny animacules."

—Dr. H. S. Browntrout
2nd. Assembly On Moral Disease
1863

Made in the USA
Columbia, SC
11 August 2018